The Old Dog and Duck

By the Same Author

Red Herrings and White Elephants
Shaggy Dogs and Black Sheep
Phantom Hitchhikers and Decoy Ducks
Loch Ness Monsters and Raining Frogs
Pop Goes the Weasel

The Old Dog and Duck

The Secret Meanings of Pub Names

Albert Jack

Illustrated by Lara Carlini

PARTICULAR
BOOKS

PARTICULAR BOOKS

Published by the Penguin Group
Penguin Books Ltd, 80 Strand, London WC2R ORL, England
Penguin Group (USA) Inc., 375 Hudson Street, New York, New York 10014, USA
Penguin Group (Canada), 90 Eglinton Avenue East, Suite 700, Toronto, Ontario,
Canada M4P 2Y3 (a division of Pearson Penguin Canada Inc.)
Penguin Ireland, 25 St Stephen's Green, Dublin 2, Ireland
(a division of Penguin Books Ltd)
Penguin Group (Australia), 250 Camberwell Road, Camberwell,
Victoria 3124, Australia (a division of Pearson Australia Group Pty Ltd)
Penguin Books India Pvt Ltd, 11 Community Centre,
Panchsheel Park, New Delhi – 110 017, India
Penguin Group (NZ), 67 Apollo Drive, Rosedale, North Shore 0632,
New Zealand (a division of Pearson New Zealand Ltd)
Penguin Books (South Africa) (Pty) Ltd, 24 Sturdee Avenue,
Rosebank, Johannesburg 2196, South Africa

Penguin Books Ltd, Registered Offices: 80 Strand, London WC2R ORL, England

www.penguin.com

First published 2009
3

Copyright © Albert Jack, 2009
Illustrations copyright © Lara Carlini, 2009
All rights reserved

The moral right of the author has been asserted

Set in 10.5/14 pt Sabon LT Std
Typeset by Palimpsest Book Production Limited, Grangemouth, Stirlingshire
Printed in England by Clays Ltd, St Ives plc

ISBN: 978-1-846-14253-6

www.greenpenguin.co.uk

This book is dedicated to
Ellie and Jack, wherever you are.
Probably in a pub.

Contents

Introduction

I rose politely in the club
And said, 'I feel a little bored;
Will someone take me to a pub?'
G. K. Chesterton

public house (*Chiefly British*) an establishment where alcoholic beverages are sold to be drunk on the premises.

And so, at last, welcome to the book I have always wanted to write. If you've read my other books, you'll know that my mission in life is tracking down the hidden meanings and secret stories behind everyday things we take for granted. Previous topics have ranged from colourful phrases (*Red Herrings and White Elephants* and *Shaggy Dogs and Black Sheep*) to nursery rhymes (*Pop Goes the Weasel*).

This time I'm writing about my favourite subject. I am a huge admirer of the British pub (and the Irish, Australian, American, South African – you name it – varieties). There's something about a good old honest-to-God boozer that can't be beaten, and so I decided to find out more about where they've come from and what their names mean. Have you ever wondered, for instance, why there should be a painting of a headless lady hanging outside the **Quiet Woman**, or of a knotted bit of rope outside the **Turk's Head,** or an executioner's axe by the **Three Lords?** It turns out that behind virtually every inn sign there is a fascinating story.

The history of pubs

As long as there has been alcohol, people have gathered together to drink it. Many pub names offer helpful signposts to the very long history of communal drinking in the British Isles. Archaeologists have found evidence of brewing in the Middle East dating as far back as the eighth century BC. Although brewing in Europe goes as far back as 3000 BC, sadly they haven't yet found any Druid watering holes (the **Standing Stone?**).

So, officially, it was the industrious Romans, after they invaded in AD 43, who first began to establish *tabernae* ('huts' or 'shops' – the origin of our word 'tavern') along their new road networks. These provided food, drink and accommodation for workers, soldiers and travellers alike. They were the alcoholic equivalent of today's motorway service stations. The Romans traditionally despised beer as the drink of the conquered indigenous peoples of Britain: their tipple of choice was wine. The weather in Britain was much warmer then and vines and wine-making flourished, even if the locals preferred their own homebrew. When the *taberna* was fully stocked with wine, some grapes would be displayed outside the building by way of an advert (the **Bunch of Grapes** – or **Crooked Billet** if the birds got there first).

After their empire began to crumble early in the fifth century and the Romans decamped back to Italy, the Anglo-Saxons then took charge. Many of the larger

Roman-established towns were abandoned and people moved into much smaller villages and settlements. Unlike their Mediterranean predecessors, the new settlers came from colder, more northerly climes and their drink of choice was ale. (Ale, incidentally, before the importation of hops in the fifteenth century, was the English term for beer.) The oldest alcoholic drink on the planet, beer has historically been seen in a much more positive light than it is today. For instance, the Mesopotamian story explaining how man evolved from the beasts and became civilized involved his being given lots of beer by a god.

Ale was central to the Anglo-Saxon sense of community. One person in the village would brew it and his home would become the local drinking spot, mustering place and centre for gossip. In a precursor of the modern pub sign, the Saxon brewer would fix a green bush (often also the source of berries for flavouring the beer) outside his house to show the ale was ready for drinking (the **Bush**). These alehouses became so popular that in 965 King Edgar decreed that they should be restricted to one per village.

When the Normans took over in 1066, they were keen to impose order on their new domain, mainly so they could work out just how much tax they could get away with demanding (the point behind the Domesday Book) and for a couple of hundred years at least they ignored alehouses. The kings concentrated on building new towns and castles; it was the Church that redeveloped the idea of the Roman *tabernae*. A network of monasteries all over the British Isles created guest-houses to offer lodging and refreshment to pilgrims. Many monasteries were renowned for the ale they brewed and for the quality of their entertainment. Contemporary depictions of monks (think of **Friar Tuck**) often showed them bingeing on food and drink. The **Dove** (the biblical symbol of peace – the bird returning to the ark with the first green shoot, marking the end of the flood and God's anger with mankind) was commonly used as a sign for a monastic guest-house.

As the Middle Ages continued and Crusades and pilgrimages became increasingly popular (**Ye Olde Trip to Jerusalem**), the monasteries couldn't cope with the demand and enterprising locals set up inns nearby. Their signs (to draw in a largely illiterate clientele of pilgrims and travellers) may well have mimicked easily recognizable images from the decorations inside churches, such as the **Lamb**, the **Ark** and various martyred saints (the **Crown and Arrows**). These hostelries were a large step up from scruffy local alehouses and some became celebrated landmarks. There is an area of north London named after a famous medieval inn, the **Angel**.

In 1393 a law was passed that all landlords must identify their premises with a sign: 'Whoever shall brew ale in town with the intention of selling it must hang out a sign, otherwise he shall forfeit his ale.' The principal reason for the legislation was so that the royal ale-tasters could easily identify pubs when they arrived in a village or hamlet in order to inspect the quality of the ale and to collect any taxes due. It made sense for a landlord to display a popular image that could easily be remembered, and many early pub names can be identified from this period, such as the **Plough**, the **Star** and the **Tabard** (a tabard was a sleeveless jacket – a loose-fitting medieval bodywarmer – which was worn by everyone, from ploughmen to knights). The Tabard in Southwark was the famous inn (sadly burned down in 1669) where Chaucer's pilgrims set off on their journey in *The Canterbury Tales*.

The Crusades and the popularity of chivalry had triggered huge interest in the legends of St George and King Arthur. Following his father's disastrous reign, Edward III looked to these old stories for inspiration in his re-branding of the monarchy (and the ruling classes). He gathered together a band of special knights (the **Star and Garter**), much in the manner of King Arthur, and chose a patron saint for England who embodied the knightly virtues he so admired (the **George and Dragon**). He also encouraged the use of heraldry, which had a knock-on effect on the names of pubs. Every noble family had its own coat of arms, and alehouses and inns on their lands were often named after them, such as the **Red Lion**, the **White Hart** and the **Bear and Ragged Staff**.

But things were far from that simple. These were turbulent times: feudalism had been destroyed by the Black Death and, much to the horror of the ruling classes, working men were demanding a better life. Alehouses were the places they gathered to complain of their lot and plot their uprisings. Although the Peasants' Revolt of 1381 was soon squashed, the changes it set in motion couldn't be suppressed as easily. The English hero the working classes chose as their favourite symbol was very different from King Arthur. **Robin Hood** was an outlaw who robbed from the rich and gave it all to the poor. To call your hostelry after him was thumbing your nose at the noble families who owned most of England and consequently most of England's pubs. To this day, the pubs named after Robin Hood outnumber those named after King Arthur ten to one.

When Henry VIII divorced his first wife in 1533 and started dissolving the monasteries, some innkeepers (canny businessmen) rushed to change the names of their inns if they seemed a little too religious to something ostensibly more loyal, such as the **King's Arms**. Meanwhile others started spinning different stories to account for their pub's name. But with the loss of the monasteries, supply was soon outstripped by demand and there was an explosion of new pubs of all different kinds and with all different kinds of name.

At the same time, Dutch and Flemish immigrants introduced hops into the brewing process and brought a new drink on to the market – 'beer'. The addition of hops gave it a distinctively bitter taste and helped it keep much longer. However, not everyone welcomed this new-age drink, regarding the addition of *hoppes* as a bad thing. Imagine how they'd have reacted to lager. Hop gardens (the **Hop Pole**) sprang up throughout southern counties such as Kent and Sussex. Henry VIII tried to stop the brewing of this new type of ale through heavy taxation but that didn't work, and so, like governments ever since, he simply trousered the money and left things alone.

Different pubs for different purposes

With pubs cropping up everywhere, things became much more complicated. Luckily that's something that can be explained by the choice of suffix. 'Tavern', 'Inn', 'Hotel' and 'Public House' each indicated a specific type of drinking hole. The early taverns in England were privately owned and thus open only to certain guests or 'members', unlike the public houses. They are perhaps the forefather of the gentleman's (or working man's) club. An inn differed from a tavern in that it was usually located along the ever-growing road network, providing overnight accommodation, food and shelter for the travellers' horses (**Coach and Horses**). These were rather grander establishments, often found in remote locations, in which the local community actually grew up around the inn. The public house, as its name suggests, grew out of the alehouses. These were local hostelries that had all the homely welcome of a private house but were open to all customers. Hotels primarily provided accommodation and were granted longer licensing hours, including on a Sunday, by catering for the long-distance traveller who would be arriving and departing at all hours of the day and night. Many early pubs labelled themselves hotels simply to benefit from the more lenient laws. Calling itself a hotel gave a pub the legal right to open for business on the Sabbath, even when the only real place it provided for sleeping was face down in the beer garden.

The Church and the pub had by now very much parted company as it became harder and harder to stop people from skipping church to spend as much time as possible drunkenly socializing. The spirit of Oliver Cromwell, who banned football, alcohol and Christmas after winning the English Civil War in 1651, held sway in Scotland until as recently as 1976 when the law finally allowed the nation, known to enjoy a wee dram, to open its public houses on the day of the Lord. Apparently it has always been fine to cut one another to pieces in the name of religion, but to have a beer or two on the prescribed day of rest was regarded as a sin. Considering that Christ's best friends were fishermen and sailors (equally famous for their love of a drink) and that his legendary ability to turn water into wine would have stood him in good stead behind any bar, I reckon he would have been happy with mankind drinking alcohol on any day it chose.

Popular history

Pub names are often celebrations of the most colourful characters and moments from our past. The **Royal Oak**, for example, is a reminder of Charles II hiding in an oak tree while escaping Cromwell's forces after the Battle of Worcester in September 1651. The **Balaclava** was not named after the woolly headgear favoured by bank robbers but a crucial battle that proved a turning point in the Crimean War. **Jack Straw's Castle** tells the story of the now forgotten joint leader of the Peasants' Revolt, which almost brought communism to England in the fourteenth century. And there are many, many more.

Hundreds, if not thousands, of pubs all over the world are named in honour of famous figures from the past. Some, such as the **Nelson** and the **Duke of Wellington** (or **Iron Duke**), remain well known today, while others have all but faded into obscurity. I'd need several volumes to cover every historical figure who ever inspired a pub name, but I wanted to give you some interesting examples of some of the men, respected enough during their own century, for their names to still be written in big letters on a building in many of our towns and cities. And yet most of us today have no real idea who they are. Pubs like the **Admiral Collingwood** and the **Prince Blucher** are named after forgotten military heroes without whom Nelson and Wellington would not have won the Napoleonic Wars, despite what your history teacher told you.

Alcohol and gambling have always gone hand in hand, but the connection between sport and pubs goes much deeper than a group of peasants gathering to bet on a cockfight (the **Cock**) or throw sticks at a ball (the **Aunt Sally**). Like the Angel at Islington, some pubs have become local landmarks. For example, there was once a Mr Ball, again over Islington way, who ran an establishment with a pond at the back filled with ducks. For a fee, drinkers could go outside and take a shot at the birds, and Balls Pond became a regular retreat for gun enthusiasts. His drinking house, no doubt named the **Old Dog and Duck**, no longer exists, but Balls Pond Road remains a busy thoroughfare in that part of London, thanks to the pub.

Many British sports evolved out of their connections with pubs. The rules of cricket were thrashed out by the Hambledon Club in the 1760s at the **Bat and Ball Inn**, where their team captain, Richard Nyren, was the landlord. The split between rugby and football (once the same game) was agreed in the **Freemasons Arms** in Covent Garden in 1863. One thing that has surprised me in my researches is just how many pubs are named after racehorses: I've added a list of my ten favourites to entertain you at the back of the book.

Terrible jokes

Pubs are also the focus of terrible joke-telling, as many names bear testament (see the **Drunken Duck** and the **Quiet Woman**, for starters). I started writing an entry about the **Dew Drop Inn** – it's a pun on 'do drop in' – but found I was losing the will to live and had to stop. It just isn't funny now, proving that joke names like this don't always stand up to the test of time. It shows too how the spirit that lies behind the modern chain pub names that make jokes about firkins (a measure of beer) and tups (sheep) is far from new.

There are often several theories behind the name of a pub and I've included all those that seem to hold water or are particularly entertaining. Yet the same name can have confusingly different origins: of two pubs called the **Case is Altered** one might be referring to a famous legal battle, while the other could be a corruption of a Spanish term for 'house of dancing' (*casa de saltar*), but that's all part of the joy of the hunt.

My only regret is that there are so many names and stories I can't include simply because I haven't got the space here to cover them. If you know a great story like the one behind the **Bucket of Blood**, the **Flying Dutchman** or **Molly Malone's**, then do please let me know (at www.albertjack.com). I'm always keen to hear the story of a local that I have yet to stumble upon, or out of. And I'm already looking forward to embarking on another six-month pub crawl (I mean research study).

The pub was once described by seventeenth-century diarist Samuel Pepys as the 'heart of England while the church is its soul'. These days I would say he is only half right. There remain over 56,000 pubs in Great Britain, half of which are filled with youngsters who play loud music on a jukebox that sounds like somebody is hitting his lawnmower with a hammer, while the next-door neighbour shouts at him over the fence. The other half, however, are the perfect place to while away an afternoon with a pint and fine conversation while quietly contemplating what to do next. Well, that's what I do anyway.

So take a seat in your favourite armchair by the fireside and join me on a pub crawl along memory lane and around history corner. We may be some time.

Acknowledgements

Special thanks to Ama and Grace Page for restoring some calm this year and reminding me of my place in the natural order of the household – last. But thanks also to Bessie, Herbert and especially Cricket for enabling me to feel superior in some small way.

Big thanks also to Robert Smith of the Robert Smith Literary Agency in London. This year, for the first time, I have nothing to thank Peter Gordon for. Perhaps he can put that right next year. Thank you, Aaliya Syed, for some last-minute research and Lara Carlini for all the illustrations.

The Penguin team also receive huge credit for all their effort and hard work. That's my editor, Georgina Laycock, copy-editor Kate Parker and the Particular Books team of Helen Conford, Ruth Stimson and Alice Dawson; my publicist, Thi Dinh, cover designer Richard Green, book designer Lisa Simmonds, the production team of Ruth Pinkney and Taryn Jones, marketeer Jessie Price, worldwide rights manager Sarah Hunt Cooke and, of course, the brilliant Penguin sales department.

In this case it is only right to mention the staff at the Fat Cactus in Cape Town, my own favourite bar. Dimo Papachristodoulou (that sounds Greek to me), Celeste Perry, Lawrence Davis – the architect of the Albert Jack shooter (and yes, I did worry about that too, until I drank it) – Candice Kalil, Ryan Rossouw and Gareth Davis, Troy Kyle, my favourite writer and apparently an Anglican minister, and last but not least Tara Hood.

Finally to you, my reader. I hope you enjoy discovering as much as I have the surprising history behind the culture that we all take so much for granted.

Albert Jack
Cape Town
June 2009

The Addison Arms

Now almost forgotten, his works barely read, Joseph Addison (1672–1719) was in his day a hugely influential author, whose writings inspired the rise of the middle classes in Britain (intentionally) and sparked revolution in America (unintentionally).

Addison met his lifelong friend Richard Steele (1672–1729) at Charterhouse School in Surrey in the 1690s and their intellectual partnership was to bring them fame and success. Addison and Steele were obsessed with the follies and foibles of their fellow countrymen and how to improve society. When they set up the *Spectator* in 1711, their stated goal was 'to enliven morality with wit, and to temper wit with morality . . . to bring philosophy out of the closets and libraries, schools and colleges, to dwell in clubs and assemblies, at tea-tables and coffeehouses'. Catering for the interests and concerns of the newly emerging middle classes, the *Spectator* was a huge success: Addison calculated that it was read by 60,000 Londoners, a tenth of the population of the city at the time.

In 1712 Addison wrote his most famous work, *Cato, a Tragedy*, a play based upon the life of the Roman politician and statesman. Cato the Younger (95–46 BC) was the implacable foe of Julius Caesar and a famously stubborn defender of republicanism: when Caesar conquered the Senate, Cato committed suicide rather than live in a country ruled by a tyrant. The play enjoyed a long run throughout Britain, Ireland and the New World and many believe it was the literary inspiration for the American War of Independence over half a century later (see also THE JOHN PAUL JONES and THE MOLLY PITCHER).

The war had many causes but prime among them was the British government's demands for huge taxes while denying its colony any political voice or influence. The Founding Fathers who saw Addison's play were understandably enthusiastic about it, dealing as it did with themes of individual liberty versus tyranny, republicanism versus monarchy, and showing its hero's determination to cleave to his beliefs come what may. George Washington is known to have had *Cato* performed before his Continental Army while the soldiers were encamped for the winter of 1777 at Valley Forge. They must have been duly roused by it as the next summer saw their decisive victory over the British.

Interestingly, many well-known quotations from the American Revolution echo lines from Addison's tragedy, such as Patrick Henry's 'Give me Liberty, or give me Death' or the immortal words of Nathan Hale (America's first spy and a national hero): 'I regret that I have but one life to lose for my country.' Addison had written, much earlier, in his play (Act 4, Scene 4): 'What a pity it is / That we can die but once to serve our country.' History had turned Addison's fiction into fact. Which would have horrified the wit who once famously said: 'we are growing serious, and let me tell you, that's the next step to being dull.'

The Admiral Collingwood
THE FORGOTTEN HERO OF THE BATTLE OF TRAFALGAR

Admiral Collingwood (1748–1810) is another forgotten hero, celebrated today only by pub names throughout Britain and America (including the **Collingwood Arms** and the **Lord Collingwood**), but one who deserves to be rehabilitated. Not that he would have cared, mind you. His memorial reads: 'He was a typical north country-man, never duly elated by success or depressed by failure, caring little for public applause.'

Cuthbert Collingwood was born in Newcastle upon Tyne and went to sea as a volunteer at the age of eleven. In 1777 he was sent to the West Indies where he met Horatio NELSON (see also THE ADMIRAL DUNCAN), serving as a lieutenant on the same ship, and they began a lifelong friendship. Both men were noted for their ambition and their courage. Their stories are intertwined but history has only remembered Nelson even though Collingwood was arguably Nelson's equal or even his superior in seaman-ship and strategic thinking.

In 1775, at the age of twenty-seven, Collingwood dis-tinguished himself at the Battle of Bunker Hill at the start of the American War of Independence. His subsequent rise through the naval ranks was as impressive as Nelson's over the following years, and by 1783 the two friends were commanding their own vessels, working together to pre-vent American ships from trading in the West Indies.

Collingwood established his reputation as a fighting commander at the Battle of Cape St Vincent in 1797 on board HMS *Excellent*. In 1803, at the beginning of the

Napoleonic Wars, he blockaded the French fleet at Brest in north-west France and the following year was promoted to vice admiral in command of a squadron tasked with harassing the French navy at every opportunity.

In 1805 Collingwood encountered sixteen French and Spanish warships close to Cadiz at the mouth of the Mediterranean. By hoisting a series of misleading flag messages, he managed to fool his opponents into believing he commanded many more ships than the three he had and thus succeeded in blockading the port completely as, fearing a vast enemy fleet was waiting for them just over the horizon, the French refused to leave the safety of Cadiz. Soon, Collingwood was joined by Nelson and between them they laid the plans to trap the enemy along the coast at Trafalgar, Nelson leading one column of warships and Collingwood the other. It was Collingwood who engaged the enemy first, inspiring Nelson to comment: 'See how that noble fellow Collingwood carries his ship into battle' (words subsequently engraved on the Collingwood Monument at Tynemouth).

When Nelson himself was famously shot dead during the early stages of the battle, Collingwood assumed total command of the fleet as the action thundered all around. He made several crucial alterations to Nelson's battle-plans and ultimately led the English to their finest hour. Had the Battle of Trafalgar been lost by the Royal Navy, Napoleon and his 120,000 troops based at Boulogne, northern France, would have been carried across the Channel to invade England in the very ships Collingwood and Nelson had destroyed at Trafalgar. While historians correctly emphasize the importance of Nelson's role in the battle, it is clear the two men were partners.

Collingwood never retired from the navy, despite growing ill health and repeatedly requesting to be relieved of his command. The government of the day refused on the grounds that his country needed him, and so he passed away in service, dying of cancer on board his ship off Port Mahon on 7 March 1810. As a result he never made it back to Collingwood House at Morpeth near Newcastle, which must have saddened the admiral, who was never happiest than when walking his dog through his estate with a pocket full of acorns. These he would plant wherever he found a good site for a fine oak tree, so that the Royal Navy would never lack the wood to build warships for the defence of the realm. Fittingly, he is buried alongside Nelson in St Paul's Cathedral.

The Admiral Duncan

CURMUDGEONLY SEADOG WHO THREW THE NAVAL RULE
BOOK OUT OF THE PORTHOLE

THE ADMIRAL
DUNCAN

The most famous of the many pubs in Britain going by this name can be found on Old Compton Street in Soho. The pub became notorious in 1999 as one of three locations around London in which a lunatic former member of the National Socialist Movement detonated a number of nail bombs. Three people lost their lives at the pub and many more were badly injured. The other Admiral Duncans around Britain have had a far more peaceful history, fortunately, although that is in direct contrast to the man they are named after.

Adam Duncan (1731–1804) was only fifteen years old when he joined the Royal Navy in 1746. His rise through the ranks was meteoric and he reached the rank of commander at the age of twenty-eight. But there he stuck as he was a difficult man and not popular with the admiralty. It took nearly forty years before Duncan finally arrived, in 1795, at the rank of commander-in-chief in the North Sea, with the responsibility of protecting Britain from the troublesome Dutch. Two years later, in the autumn of 1797, it was Admiral Duncan who prevented the Dutch fleet, at that time commanded by the French, from invading Ireland and establishing a new threat to Britain from the west. Tearing up the established rule book of naval warfare, Duncan ordered his fleet to sail directly at the Dutch lines, instead of the more conventional, and gentlemanly, approach from the side.

This celebrated encounter, known as the Battle of Camperdown, brought immediate fame for Duncan and he returned to London a national hero, was honoured everywhere he went and given the freedom of both London and his home town of Dundee, in Scotland. In Newcastle upon Tyne there is a pub called the **Camperdown** in memory of Duncan's victory. Meanwhile, in the same year a much younger officer, one Horatio NELSON, had a similar job tackling the French and Spanish in the Mediterranean, distinguishing himself at the Battle of Cape Vincent (see also THE ADMIRAL COLLINGWOOD). It was to be another eight years before Britain's most renowned naval hero dealt with the French and Spanish navies by copying Duncan's tactics at Camperdown, sailing directly at the Franco-Spanish fleet and scattering their ships in all directions before winning one of the most famous battles in history, close to the coast of a small Spanish cape called Trafalgar.

The Admiral Vernon
THE HERO OF THE WAR OF JENKINS' EAR

Edward Vernon (1684–1757) made his career, in the style of his hero Sir Francis Drake (see THE GOLDEN HIND), out of harassing the Spanish, and was present during the capture of Gibraltar (1704) and Barcelona (1705), as well as seeing action during the Battle of Malaga on 24 August 1704.

In 1728 tentative peace was made with Spain, but this didn't last long and Vernon was once again despatched to sort out the Spanish. The renewal of hostilities was all down to one Robert Jenkins, a merchant seaman who claimed his ship had been boarded in the West Indies by the Spanish coastguard, who had tied him to the mast and cut off his ear with a sword, threatening to do the same to the King of England if he ever had the chance. In 1738

Jenkins presented his severed ear to Parliament and they in turn were provoked enough to declare a new war against Spain, sending Vernon, now promoted to vice admiral, to the West Indies with a small fleet to test the Spanish defences.

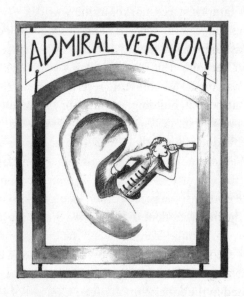

Vernon's first act in what became known as the War of Jenkins' Ear (1739–42) was to seize Portobelo, a silver-exporting port on the Spanish-held coast of Panama. His men occupied the port for three weeks, completely destroying its defensive positions before withdrawing. The Spanish economy had been dealt a severe blow from which it would take years to recover. News of Vernon's actions was enthusiastically received in London. Places were named in celebration of the victory, including a farm in what is now Notting Hill and the country road running from it: Portobello Lane. In 1740, at a society dinner in honour of the admiral, 'Rule Britannia' (see THE BRITANNIA) was performed for the first time, stirring up great national pride. Over time Portobello Lane became, of course, Portobello Road, one of the best-known London street names and the location of possibly the most famous street market in the world.

During the War of Jenkins' Ear, a sailor called Lawrence Washington was fighting in an American regiment as part of Vernon's fleet (America being still a British colony at that time). Washington received notice from his father that he was building a house for him overlooking the Potomac River at Alexandria, Virginia. The young sailor replied that his father should name the new house Mount Vernon in honour of the admiral. After Lawrence Washington's death in 1752, the Mount Vernon estate passed over to his younger brother, George, who in 1789 became the first President of the United States of America, returning to Mount Vernon when he retired in 1797. Mount Vernon was designated by the American government a National Historic Landmark in 1960, as well as being listed in the American National Register of Historic Places. It stands today as a proud memorial to the first president and a reminder of one of England's greatest naval commanders. But that isn't Vernon's only legacy.

By 1740 the admiral was a well-known figure, easily recognized by his trademark grogram or grosgrain coat (it was a coarse mixture of mohair and silk), earning himself the affectionate nickname 'Old Grog'. During the War of Jenkins' Ear, Vernon had ordered that all rum rations, issued to the sailors twice daily, be watered down, possibly in an attempt to prevent drunken ill-discipline. The rum was also to be laced with lime or lemon juice to prevent scurvy. It wasn't long before the entire British navy followed suit. In response, in 1781, Thomas Trotter, a sailor on board the *Berwick*, wrote the following poem about Vernon and his Portobelo flagship:

> A mighty bowl on deck he drew
> And filled it to the brink;
> Such drank the *Burford*'s gallant crew
> And such the gods shall drink.
>
> The sacred robe which Vernon wore
> Was drenched within the same;
> And hence his virtues guard our shore,
> And Grog derives its name.

The unhappy sailors of the fleet soon began calling the watered-down ration 'grog' and as an extension of that drunken sailors were labelled 'groggy'.

In 1746 Old Grog retired from active service and spent the rest of his days concentrating on politics and naval affairs. His lasting monuments remain Mount Vernon, home of America's first president, Portobello Road in London and his name on many English pubs that will do their level best to help you feel 'groggy' the next morning.

The Agincourt

ONCE MORE UNTO THE BREACH, DEAR FRIENDS

In 1414 a generation of English and Frenchmen had taken a twenty-six-year break from slaughtering each other. They were already seventy-seven years into the Hundred Years'

The Agincourt

War (although the Hundred and Sixteen Years' War would be a more accurate name), which could have been a few decades shorter had the young English king, Henry V, not turned down the French invitation to resolve their territorial differences. Claiming Charles VI's offer of settlement was insulting, Henry gathered his troops together and in August 1415 landed his army on the Normandy coastline, intending to head for Paris.

But a rethink was needed after his siege of the port of Harfleur took six weeks, far longer than expected. By the time the town had surrendered, on 22 September, autumn was closing in and the season for mindless violence was all but over, so Henry started back towards Calais, at that time an English stronghold, to regroup and re-arm for the following spring.

The Siege of Harfleur had given the French time to react, however, and troops were already marching north to confront the English at the Somme, in northern France, an area made famous many centuries later as the scene of far greater slaughter, during the First World War (see THE LORD KITCHENER). After a three-week march of over 260 miles the English army was weak, ill and hoping to reach the safety of Calais instead of being drawn into a pitched battle. With an army of under 9,000, its numbers depleted by disease and desertion, Henry had no intention of attacking the French. But he was forced into action when, on 24 October, enemy troops caught up with and trapped his men on a narrow strip of land in a forest between Agincourt and Tramecourt.

Things looked pretty bad for the English. Early the following day Henry addressed his men, pointing out to them that each and every one was in a fight for his life, as prisoners were unlikely to be taken. The French, by contrast, greater in number and occupying a better battle position, were confident of a quick victory, believing they could wipe out the English threat and head home before winter set in.

But the English had one trick up their sleeve: the longbow. Equivalent in length to the height of the individual archer, the bow had already proved its worth at the Battle of Crécy in 1346 (see THE STAR AND GARTER). Henry knew that, used en masse, the weapon could be deployed at a long range, devastating an entire army from two hundred yards away, while the archers remained at a relatively safe distance from the enemy. The king therefore deployed 5,000 longbowmen at his flanks, the vast majority of his army, who dug in behind rows of sharpened pikes. They were protected from the cavalry charge of the French knights by the thick forest on either side.

Once his bowmen were ready, Henry ordered the initial attack on the French army, who must have been surprised to find themselves on the receiving end of ten arrows per archer per minute. Within ten minutes of the first volley, half a million arrows had shattered the French lines, causing mayhem and panic. French knights charged the archers only to find themselves caught between the spiked defences and more horsemen coming up behind. Trapped directly in front of the archers and weighed down by their heavy armour, they were scythed down within minutes and the English foot soldiers, wielding swords and hatchets, then moved in to finish them off.

When the archers ran out of arrows, they dropped their bows and waded into the fray with axes, and soon up to 10,000 Frenchmen lay dead, against English losses of only 1,600, although some historians claim that was the overall number of the wounded and only 100 Englishmen actually lost their lives. Either way, Agincourt was a major victory for the English and a disaster for the French as most of their knights and military leaders were killed, severely restricting French military capability for a generation to follow.

Agincourt is celebrated in pub names throughout Britain and in Shakespeare's rousing play *Henry V*. The Laurence Olivier film that came out in 1944 was key to raising British morale in the darkest days of the Second World War. But the really interesting thing is the way the French remember it . . .

For a town with such a huge and historic reputation, Agincourt – or Azincourt, as the French call it – is a remarkably nondescript little place with a population of just under 300. Even so, the French hold an annual festival there, including re-enactments of the battle, to commemorate their crushing defeat by the English longbowmen. What a strange thing to do! If the French were to hold a festival to commemorate every important battle they have lost, then there would be one every day of the year.

The Albion

THERE'LL BE SYRIAN PRINCESSES OVER THE WHITE CLIFFS OF DOVER

Albion is an ancient and romantic name for Britain that some believe evolved from the Latin word *albus* (meaning 'white') in reference to the famous cliffs at Dover and Seaford that greet the traveller from mainland Europe, providing his first view of the country. Ancient Britain was occupied by a series of tribes who all had different

THE ALBION

names for the areas that they lived in; it was the traders and the potential invaders who needed to name the whole place, generally basing what they called it on the small amount of knowledge they had of the country. White cliffs apart, it is equally possible that the name Albion for the British Isles could have arisen from 'Albany' – derived from the Gaelic word 'Alba' – the ancient name for the northern part of Scotland, later renamed Caledonia by the Romans (see THE BRITANNIA).

The name found on many a pub sign throughout Britain could derive from another source, however – classical mythology. Albion, the giant son of Neptune, the Roman god of the sea, is said to have discovered the islands and ruled over them for forty-four years. But according to another legend, 'Albion' has more female connotations. The fifty daughters of the King of Syria all married on the same day and marked the occasion by murdering their husbands on the communal wedding night. As punishment they were all set adrift in a ship and finally ran ashore on the coast of what is now known as Britain. Here they established a colony and each daughter, the eldest of whom was called Albia, married local natives and formed their own community of Albions, never to return to their homeland.

In 1579 Sir Francis Drake, the great Elizabethan explorer (see THE GOLDEN HIND), annexed an area of land now known as California during his circumnavigation of the globe and claimed it for the Virgin Queen. He marked this discovery with a brass plaque naming the territory New Albion and this plate, it is recorded, eventually turned up somewhere near San Francisco in 1937, but by then Old Albion had seen what the settlers were doing to the place and decided they didn't want it after all.

The Alma
THE WAR TO NAME ALL PUBS

There are many inns around Britain bearing this name, or a variation of it. The **Battle of Alma**, **Heroes of Alma**, **Heights of Alma** and the **Alma Arms** are just a few examples. The Alma is the name of the major river running through the area of the Ukraine formerly known as the Crimea. On 20 September 1854 it became the scene of the first key battle of the Crimean War, fought by the British and her European allies against the Russians over lands once occupied by the declining Ottoman Empire.

The result was a stunning, if unexpected, victory for Britain and France during one of the few periods of history when the two countries were actually on the same side and not fighting each other. This triumph was marked all over Britain with references to the Alma, and hundreds of returning soldiers called their newborn daughters Alma out of respect for their fallen comrades, leading to a Ukrainian river becoming one of the most popular girls' names of the late nineteenth century.

The Battle of Alma led directly to the Russian counter-offensive a month later at Balaclava, which became famous for the ill-fated Charge of the Light Brigade, led by Lord Cardigan under the command of Lieutenant General George Charles Bingham (1800–88), otherwise known as the 3rd Earl of Lucan. He was the less-than-illustrious ancestor of the rather more notorious Richard John Bingham (1934–?), 7th Earl of Lucan, missing since 1974 and still wanted by the police. (If you could check the quieter corners of your local pub for him –

he'd be getting on a bit now, of course – they'd be most grateful.)

Like the knitted headcovering with holes for eyes, nose and mouth (it was bitterly cold in the Crimean Peninsular) so favoured by today's bankrobbers, pubs in Britain were named the **Balaclava** in honour of the men who fought there, and the 350 British soldiers who lost their lives on that day. It was the disaster at Balaclava, caused by the incompetence of the commanding officers, that led the British army to review the practice of selling commissions to wealthy noblemen, enabling them to buy any rank they could afford and, without any special training, lead soldiers into battle. This led to the Cardwell Reforms, established between 1868 and 1874, that also banned flogging and branding as a form of punishment in both the army and the navy.

Aldershot, for many years the home of the British army, also has a pub in honour of the campaign. It is called, quite simply, the **Crimea,** and locals even go to the lengths of re-enacting, with convincing realism, some of the more violent scenes of the historic conflict every weekend. At least that's what it looked like to me when I drove past there the other night.

The Anchor
WHAT SHALL WE DO WITH THE THIRSTY SAILOR?

There are two main theories why the anchor is such a popular symbol for a pub. The principal, and most likely, reason why the name or image adorns alehouses and taverns across the land (see THE HOPE AND ANCHOR for the other one) is based on the notion that sailors are legendary drinkers, famous for spending several months' wages on one night out. The pubs of the port towns or city docks would display an anchor outside their premises to attract sailors, in the hope that, after setting foot on land for the first time in months, maybe even years, they would be thirsty for ale and put away as much as they could. And, needless to say, that's what many of them did.

Variations on the theme, such as the **Anchor and Horsehoes**, are more likely to have been a combination of two names after a business had changed hands. Other examples include the **Royal Anchor**, if a member of the royal family had ever paid a visit, the **Crown and Anchor**, if that had been a ruling monarch, or the **Golden Anchor**. Meanwhile, some inland examples of the Anchor are thought to have non-nautical origins, such as the 'anchor man' in a local tug-of-war team or the anchors used to hold down hot air balloons before and after take-off.

My favourite Anchor can be found in an area of Bristol known as the 'Made Forever'. The story goes that two local miners, Lewis and Fudge, discovered a huge seam of coal and exclaimed: 'That's it, we are made for ever!' The blacksmith's forge opposite the pub was famous for making ships' anchors and hence the pub became known as the **Anchor Made Forever**.

The Aunt Sally
FORGET WORZEL GUMMIDGE . . .

Originally a pub or fairground game of throwing something at a target, the phrase became used metaphorically to mean something or someone set up as a target for criticism. Much like myself.

In fairgrounds and pubs across the land, Aunt Sally was something to be set up simply in order to be knocked down again, proving conclusively that the British press were not the first to think up the idea. Aunt Sally consisted originally of the moulded head of a lady sporting a clay pipe in her mouth, which evolved over the years into a ball on a stake, similar to the coconut shies of more recent times. The idea was for participants to knock the pipe from the lady's mouth, in a rather more benign reinvention of the 'sport' it derived from (animal lovers should look away now) in which a cock was tied to a post and weighted sticks were thrown at the poor bird until somebody killed it. The winner took it home to cook. (The squeamish among you can look again.)

Aunt Sally is still played in pubs, often bearing the same name and sited mainly in London and the home counties of Buckinghamshire, Berkshire and Oxfordshire. Here the game consists of a ball placed on a wooden plinth. After a few drinks, locals amuse themselves by throwing sticks at the ball to try and knock it off without hitting the plinth. I have been in many pubs where locals amuse themselves after a few beers by throwing anything they can get their hands on (and it can be inspirational – see J. D. WETHERSPOON). I have never heard it called Aunt Sally before, so I am planning a trip to Oxfordshire to find out a little more . . .

The Bag of Nails

THE ULTIMATE IN DIY ACCOMMODATION OR DRUNKEN
REVELS WITH A GOD?

Some people have argued that this pub name comes from
a hoary old joke where a man walks into a pub and asks
for a room. The sign says that it's one shilling for the
night or sixpence if you make your own bed. When the
man chooses to make his own bed, the landlord gives
him some wood and a bag of nails . . .

The Bag of Nails sounds a very utilitarian name for a
pub but a fascinating theory about its origins comes all
the way from classical mythology. The name (try saying it
fast a couple of times) could well be a corruption of bac-
chanals, which were the celebrations of the Roman god of
wine. Bacchus wasn't just the god of wine, however, he
was also the god of ritual madness – and his rites were
characterized by maniacal dancing to the sound of loud
music, in which his followers, who were mostly female,
whirled around, screamed, became drunk and incited one
another to greater and greater ecstasy. The goal was to
achieve a state of enthusiasm in which their souls were
temporarily freed from their earthly bodies and able to
commune with Bacchus. The rite climaxed in a perform-
ance of frenzied feats of strength and madness, such as
uprooting trees, tearing a bull (the god's symbol) apart
with their bare hands and eating its flesh raw. Some of
you may be now be nodding your heads, realizing there
must be rather more going on than meets the eye on a
Saturday night at the Bag of Nails.

Bacchus is easy to blame for high-spirited revelries

that get out of hand and are best forgotten the next day.

However, this theory is strongly denied by the history of a specific pub, the Bag of Nails close to Buckingham Palace in London. The pub first opened in 1774 shortly after George III bought the Duke of Buckingham's London home (not the duke celebrated in the eponymous pub name, but John Sheffield – see THE DUKE OF BUCKINGHAM). The story goes that the pub was converted from an ironmonger's or blacksmith's shop, the 'Nails' was thought to service the staff of King George and of his wife, Queen Charlotte. The pub name is thought to have evolved from the old ironmonger's sign, which was traditionally a bag of nails. However, this might always be the pub's owners deciding on an origin for their name that was boringly respectable rather than scandalous. Royal servants, whatever they might really get up to off duty, must be *seen* to be behaving politely.

The Bear and Ragged Staff
WATERING HOLE OF THE KINGMAKER?

Many pub signs have come about as a result of an innkeeper showing loyalty to a local landowner. The fact that signs with very specific origins can be found in other parts of the country is simply due to migration – an innkeeper moving to another region, or indeed another part of the world, and reusing the name, for instance. The Bear and Ragged Staff, widespread throughout the country, is one such example. Originally, pubs bearing this sign, the heraldic emblem of the Earl of Warwick, would have appeared only in Warwickshire. The fact that it also crops up in other parts of the country is mostly likely because it makes a good name for a pub and a striking image (the bear muzzled and chained to the staff) for a pub sign. However, there is an additional reason for its appearance outside the home county of William Shakespeare.

One of the characters in the history play *Henry VI, Part Two* is Richard Neville, the 16th Earl of Warwick (1428–71), otherwise known as the Kingmaker. In Act 5, Scene 1, Shakespeare has him say: 'Now, by my father's badge, old Neville's crest, / The rampant bear chained to the ragged staff, / This day I will wear aloft my burgonet [helmet].' According to the legend, the first Earl of Warwick killed a bear with his own hands and the second earl despatched another by using a branch torn from a tree (the 'ragged staff'), which is why bears and staffs were included in their noble coat of arms. Reference to the 'crest' in Shakepeare's play (also appearing as a prop on stage) would have made the emblem much more widely known. So it's largely thanks to the Bard that the image is still in use five hundred years later. (For the **Dog and Bear**, see THE OLD DOG AND DUCK.)

The Belvedere
HOW THE POPE'S SUMMERHOUSE INSPIRED AN ENDURING FASHION

A belvedere is a structure at the top of a building or in an elevated location – such as on a hill in a formal garden – affording a wide panoramic view. Prior to the fifteenth century, however, surveying the countryside from an elevated location wasn't something you did for leisure, especially during times of conflict. Lookouts keeping watch from a high vantage point by the sea or near a town would be relied upon to alert their fellows to any unusual activity, whether an army returning in triumph or an enemy approaching with menace. But then from the late fifteenth century, looking at the view simply for its own sake suddenly became fashionable.

'Belvedere', meaning 'beautiful view', from the Italian *bel* ('beautiful') and *vedere* ('to see'), is a term that crops up from that time. The original belvedere, a summer-house by the same name, was built on the hillside above the Vatican for Pope Innocent VIII in the late 1400s. Subsequently, the architect Donato Bramante (1444–1514) was commissioned to design a huge courtyard, the Cortile del Belvedere, to link the Villa Belvedere with the Vatican. Taking pride of place in the courtyard is an ancient statue of Apollo, rediscovered in 1489 and depicting an image of the god as a youth with his cloak thrown back to display his naked perfection. Known as the *Apollo Belvedere*, the statue was much admired and became widely copied, while the villa itself inspired a fashion for similar structures built in panoramic places.

There are now hundreds of inns, hotels and restaurants called the Belvedere, stretching from Calcutta in the east and California to the west, so if you find yourself in one, as you go about your travels, then presumably you'd be best advised to ask for a table by the window.

The Ben Jonson

DRINK TO ME ONLY WITH THINE EYES . . . ?

Those whose historical knowledge dates back only to the 1980s will be relieved to know that pubs all over Britain are not named after Ben Johnson, the American Olympic sprinter who won a gold medal at the 1988 Olympics but was later stripped of his title when he was exposed as a drugs cheat.

The real Benjamin Jonson (1572–1637) was a poet, playwright and actor. He knew all the important writers of the period, including Shakespeare, and in later life was a big influence on younger poets, who formed an early version of a fan club, called the 'Tribe of Ben' or 'Sons of Ben'. In his younger years, however, Jonson attracted quite a bit of controversy, even ending up in prison on a couple of occasions. The first spell in gaol came about following his arrest on a charge of 'leude and mutynous behaviour', due to the supposedly offensive content of a play, *The Isle of Dogs*, co-written with Thomas Nashe (1567–c.1601) and quickly suppressed. A year later, in 1598, Jonson was imprisoned again for a brief period after killing a fellow actor in a duel. Such was his fame, or notoriety, many an anecdote about him still circulates today.

One such tale relates how the writer had been avoiding his favourite tavern after falling into debt with the inn-keeper. Then one day they bumped into each other on the street and the landlord told Jonson that if he could answer four simple questions he would wipe the slate clean. Jonson agreed and the landlord posed his questions, confident the writer would struggle to answer them:

1. What pleases God?
2. What pleases the Devil?
3. What pleases everybody?
4. What pleases me?

But he had underestimated Jonson, who, after the briefest pause, wrote down his replies:

1. God is best pleased when man forsakes his sin.

2. The Devil is best pleased when man persists with them.

3. The world is best pleased when you draw them good wine.

4. And you are best pleased when I pay you for mine.

The slate was wiped clean and Jonson invited back and presented with a fine case of wine for his ready wit. This story probably isn't the reason there are pubs and hotels still named after the writer nearly four hundred years after his death, but it is a good tale nonetheless.

Jonson was appointed the king's poet in 1619, three years after Shakespeare's death, a position he retained until his own demise in 1637. His body is buried in Westminster Abbey, London.

The Bishop's Finger
SIGNPOST TO A SAINT OR A PINT OF REAL ALE?

Pubs called the Bishop's Finger were originally found only in Kent, their name commemorating the fingerposts along the Pilgrim's Way that pointed travellers in the direction of the shrine of the murdered Archbishop Thomas à Becket in Canterbury Cathedral before Henry VIII destroyed it (the shrine, that is) in 1539, during the Dissolution of the Monasteries. Bishop's Finger is now best known as the Kentish ale made by Shepherd Neame (one of Britain's oldest brewers, established in 1698) and exported throughout the world.

The Blind Beggar
THIRTEENTH-CENTURY EARL WHO WENT FROM RICHES TO RAGS

There are very few Blind Beggar pubs in Great Britain, which is not too surprising as it's hardly the most appealing of names. Except to goths and bikers, that is: the Blind Beggar pub in Edinburgh is devoted just to them.

The original Blind Beggar, in Whitechapel Road, east

The Blind Beggar

London, is by far the best known, and with the most colourful history. There has been a drinking house on the same site since at least 1664, and it was there, in 1865, that the British Methodist preacher William Booth gave the sermon that led to the formation of the Salvation Army. There was to be no salvation for the decaying building, however, as it was pulled down a few years later and rebuilt in 1894.

But the name did not change, and it was still the Blind Beggar when, on 9 March 1966, gangster Ronnie Kray calmly walked into the bar and shot rival mobster George Cornell between the eyes. No salvation for Cornell then, either, nor for Kray, who spent the rest of his life in prison for the murder, not to mention a string of unsavoury crimes committed with twin brother Reggie.

The pub's name is thought to have been inspired by a popular Elizabethan poem, 'The Ballad of Bethnal Green' (adjoining Whitechapel). It tells the tale of a poor blind beggar who sat at the crossroads with his begging box and became a well-known figure locally. Over the years the tramp's daughter, Bessie, a beautiful girl with fine manners, attracted the attention of many brave knights, all of whom rejected her when they learned of her humble origins. All of them, that is, apart from one young gentleman, who loved Bessie enough to marry her despite her lowly background. It was only after he had asked the old beggar for his daughter's hand in marriage that the tramp then admitted that his true identity was the rightful Earl of Leicester. Much to the surprise of both his daughter and her suitor, he then endowed the couple with a great fortune.

This song about a beggar who long lost his sight
And had a fair daughter most pleasant and bright,
And many a gallant brave suitor had she
Because none was so comely as pretty Bessie.

So begins the ballad and, sixty-three verses later, it concludes:

Thus was the feast ended with joy and delight;
A happy bridegroom was made the young knight,
Who lived with great joy and felicity
With his fair lady, dear pretty Bessie.

The old blind beggar turned out to be none other than Henry de Montfort, son of the Earl of Leicester, whose army had been crushed at the Battle of Evesham on 4 August 1265 by the forces of Edward I, better known as Longshanks or the Hammer of the Scots. The Earl of Leicester had been killed on the battlefield that day and his son and heir, blinded by the blade of one of the king's knights, was left for dead.

It was there that a young baroness discovered Henry, helped him from the battlefield and secretly nursed him back to health. They later travelled to London, married and produced a daughter, Bessie, a girl of fine noble stock, although the secret was kept until her marriage. And that is the message of the Blind Beggar of Bethnal Green: don't be blinded by your desire for money and position, but follow your heart and be kind. A pity that Ronnie Kray didn't follow his advice.

The Bombay Grab
(Bow, London)

SEVENTEENTH-CENTURY SEADOG MILLIONAIRES?

In 1661 the seven islands of Bombay were ceded to
Charles II in the dowry of his new, Portuguese wife,
Catherine of Braganza. Eight years later the islands were
rented to the East India Company for £10 a year (see
THE JOHN COMPANY). Based on a deep natural harbour on the west coast of India, Bombay proved the perfect trading spot and rapidly became the largest city in
India, growing by 600 per cent in just fifteen years. In
1687 the East India Company transferred its headquarters there.

The trade worked in both directions. Opium, silk, cotton and spices were imported to England, but all kinds of
British products were exported outwards on the trading
ships' return journeys. Prime among these was beer (see
THE WHEATSHEAF). This must have gone east with the
first ships from England to sail to the Indies in the sixteenth century. Because fresh water inevitably became
brackish over a long voyage, beer was the regular drink
on sailing ships. But now it wasn't just the ships that
demanded English beer; it was the growing colonies. By
1750 almost 1,500 barrels were being exported from
England to the areas governed by the East India Company, a figure that had risen to 9,000 barrels by 1800.

The shipyard of the East India Company was at Blackwall, along the Thames, downriver from the City of London and just to the west of the mouth of the River Lea.

When the commanders and captains of the East India-men – the ships chartered by the East India Company – went to buy goods to export, they turned for the beer to a brewer close by, George Hodgson, at Bow. Hodgson was an unusual choice as his was a small company, but the beer from his brewery could be transported easily to Blackwall for loading on to the East Indiamen, and, crucially, he offered a lengthy period of credit of up to eighteen months.

What really made Hodgson's name was an unexpected side effect of his beer's six-month journey out to India. By the time the beer arrived in Bombay, Madras or Calcutta, having gone via Madeira, Rio de Janeiro, St Helena, Cape Town and the stormy Mozambique Channel, his October Ale had become paler and more bitter, perfect for the unremitting heat of the Indian subcontinent, and the ancestor of today's India Pale Ale. The expatriate British running the East India Company's 'factories' and commanding its three private armies loved it, and by the beginning of the nineteenth century Hodgson's was the beer pronounced 'in almost universal use' in India. The Bow brewery's reputation was established in that country, its name now a guarantee of quality: in 1809 it was being advertised in the *Calcutta Gazette* as 'Hodgson's select Pale Ale, warranted of superior excellence'.

By 1815 over 4,000 barrels were being exported to drinkers across the British Empire, an increase in trade of over 400 per cent in just a decade. George Hodgson's son Mark moved the brewery to a new premises a few hundred yards along the river at Bow Bridge and set up a pub there. His choice of name has puzzled many. The official reason is the pub was called after the East India Company's Bombay headquarters, and a two-masted Eastern coasting-vessel known in Arabic as a *gurab*. But I prefer the more cynical suggestion that the name really celebrates the fortune they had managed to grab from Bombay.

The Britannia
WHAT DID THE ROMANS EVER DO FOR US?

Slightly over two thousand years ago, our group of islands off the north-east coast of mainland Europe was invaded twice by a well-armed and murderous group of Romans led by Julius Caesar. At the time the mainland was called ALBION, Ireland Hibernia and Scotland Caledonia, but the Romans combined them all under the umbrella name Britanniae (i.e. 'Britains', referring to all the islands). The name itself derives from the word used by the ancient Greek Pytheas in his famous account of a voyage around the islands between 330 and 320 BC.

Caesar's first invasion was short-lived but his second was more successful, despite his initial disappointment at Britain's lack of pearls, gold or silver and the discovery that tin was the most valuable metal commonly available (after all, this was two millennia before the invention of the beer can). After nearly two hundred rebellion-suppressing years with the natives, the Roman emperor Hadrian ordered a wall to be built from coast to coast to protect his army from the Picts (northern dwellers of Albion). This was when the Romans officially called the southern part of the island and their province Britannia and the area north of the wall Caledonia. Ireland, which was never occupied by the Romans, was given the name Hibernia, from which the present name, Eire, derives.

The Romans were adept at absorbing other nations into their empire and one very successful way of doing this was by integrating the gods and beliefs of their conquered peoples into their own. In the rebellious province of Britannia this was a vital policy. The local Celtic goddess Brigantia, the equivalent of Minerva, the Roman goddess of wisdom, warriors, trade and poetry, was picked to represent Britannia and Hadrian introduced coins bearing her image. In early portraits she appears as a beautiful woman in a flowing gown or toga with one breast exposed and wearing a centurion's helmet. The symbolic message to the conquered people was unmistakable: the British goddess was dressed as a Roman and all the more powerful for it. (Interestingly, the early Christian Church used a similar tactic when trying to convert the Irish, appropriating many of Brigantia's stories and symbols under the persona of the Irish saint Brigid.)

After the Roman Empire fell into decline, its former province shifted back into a series of small kingdoms and the name Britannia became less relevant. The Anglo-Saxons fighting against the encroaching Vikings (see THE DUKE OF YORK) concentrated on their own territory and identity and renamed it England, Land of the Angles, after themselves. England continued as a separate nation for the next few centuries, annexing Wales in 1284 and finally achieving union (of a sort) with Scotland, when James I (James VI of Scotland) took over the English throne in 1603. It was time for a new name for the territories and one that would unite them, but while James I often called himself the King of Great Britain, the English and the Scottish remained thoroughly separate (and hostile).

The Acts of Union of 1707 created an official United Kingdom, but it wasn't until an entirely new and entirely un-English royal family (see THE GEORGE) took over the throne in 1714 that hearts and minds began to change. England had been shaken by civil war and the Glorious Revolution, Scotland by a series of rebellions supporting various dysfunctional members of the Stuart family; a united kingdom was a necessity. As pragmatic as Hadrian before him, George I may not have been able to speak English but he clearly understood the dangers of disunity, as did his son, George II. Then help came the monarchy's way in the form of a poem drawing on the old symbolism of the proudly defiant warrior goddess uniting Britons with their Roman conquerors.

'Rule, Britannia' was written by James Thomson in 1740 and set to music by Thomas Arne to entertain Frederick, Prince of Wales at the royal court. The song was an instant success, helping to instil some much needed patriotism into the British public. Here is in slightly abridged form:

> When Britain first, at Heaven's command,
> Arose from out the azure main;
> This was the charter of the land,
> And guardian angels sang this strain:
> 'Rule, Britannia! rule the waves:
> Britons never will be slaves.'

The nations, not so blest as thee,
Must, in their turns, to tyrants fall;
While thou shall flourish great and free,
The dread and envy of them all.
'Rule, Britannia! rule the waves:
Britons never will be slaves.'

The Muses, still with freedom found,
Shall to thy happy coast repair;
Blest Isle! with matchless beauty crowned,
And manly hearts to guard the fair.
'Rule, Britannia! rule the waves:
Britons never will be slaves.'

Thanks to the song, the figure of Britannia grew in popularity. Still sporting the centurion's helmet, she was also frequently depicted holding a trident to symbolize Britain's domination of the oceans of the world. Britannia was thus adopted by the Royal Navy as a figurehead, and due to the supremacy of the British fleet her image was seen to represent Britain to the world at large. Any hint of raciness was now gone, however, as, unlike her French counterpart, Marianne, she was no longer topless.

Over the years Britannia has grown into an important and popular image that British people can easily identify with, especially at times of war. Adorning many a pub sign throughout the land, she is seen to represent freedom and democracy in the same way that 'Lady Liberty' does for the Americans. This is despite an apparent attempt by Gordon Brown to lower Britannia's profile by removing her image from coins minted from 2008. Although that should have come as no surprise, because he is, after all, Scottish.

The Bucket of Blood
(Phillack, Cornwall)

WHEN DRAWING A PINT COULD MEAN SOMETHING MORE
SINISTER...

Two hundred and fifty years ago, the number of smugglers in Britain was thought to be around 150,000. As many as 300 ships were fully employed bringing contraband goods into the coves and on to the beaches of southern England. Cornwall was the most popular choice due to its vast number of small inlets and hidden coves. It was also estimated that as much as 25 per cent of the entire import and export trade of the England during the seventeenth and eighteenth centuries consisted of smuggled goods, and duties to the king were rarely being collected. At one point the authorities in London believed the entire adult population of Cornwall was involved in smuggling, either as a consumer or an illegal importer.

The smugglers and their families were a violent and desperate bunch (seventeenth-century Cornwall must have been like living in Mafia-run Sicily), renowned for their bloodthirsty antics. Many would stop at nothing to make the maximum amount of profit, wrecking any ship that wasn't part of their network. There's an old Cornish expression, 'jibber the kibber', which refers to the tactic of fixing a lantern round the neck of a horse led along the shore at night to make it appear like a ship's light. The ships bearing towards it ran aground, their cargoes were plundered and any surviving crew murdered by the locals.

The government was extremely keen to claw back

control of England's very profitable trade and its revenue officers were under strong pressure to produce results. Officers drawn from local families would turn a blind eye to smuggling activities, but those who came from London were less tolerant of the covert behaviour of locals, and this led to conflict and violence on a regular basis.

Revenue officers were generally regarded as insensitive to the poverty of the Cornish, interested only in collecting income for themselves and their paymasters in London. In consequence, it was common for officers to be shunned at best or, at worst, go missing. No one therefore was too surprised when the landlord of the New Inn in the village of Phillack, located on a small cove close to St Ives on the northern coast of Cornwall, went to draw his morning water from the well only to find the head of an unpopular revenue man floating in a bucketful of blood. Whether this is true or not – although given what we know about smuggling, pirates and the Cornish, it very likely is – it is certainly why, in 1980, the New Inn was renamed the Bucket of Blood, possibly my favourite pub name of all.

The Bull
TALL STORIES AND PAPAL DECREES

The Bull seems a pretty self-explanatory name for a pub. A bull is, after all, the crucial possession of every dairy farmer and most Bull Inns – and variations such as the **Black Bull, Brown Bull, Red Bull, Bull's Head, Old Bull** and just about every other type of bull you can imagine – are found in farming areas, or what were once farming

areas. But there could be other reasons behind the name, ones unrelated to agriculture.

A formal proclamation by the Pope is known as a papal bull – from the *bulla* or seal attached to the official document – so in previous centuries an innkeeper choosing to call his inn the Bull may well have been displaying his loyalty as a Roman Catholic. The origin of many of the pubs called the Bull can be traced back to the time of the Reformation when, following the annulment of his marriage to Catherine of Aragon in 1533 (see THE CAT AND FIDDLE), Henry VIII defied Rome and rejected the Catholic faith. To demonstrate his defiance of the Pope and the bull threatening him with excommunication, Henry included a bull's head on his coat of arms, reflecting his fondness for cutting off the heads of those who displeased him. So it is quite possible that all pubs formerly calling themselves the Bull's Head did so out of loyalty to King Henry VIII, while those named the Bull may have instead been showing their allegiance to the man in the dress in the Vatican.

Another meaning may come from the name of the figure that personifies England, John Bull, represented as a stout, red-faced man, dressed in a shallow top hat, waistcoat and tails and often accompanied by a bulldog. The American author Washington Irving described him, and hence the typical Englishman, as a

> plain, downright, matter-of-fact fellow . . . There is little of romance in his nature, but a vast deal of a strong natural feeling. He excels in humor more than in wit; is jolly rather than gay; melancholy rather than morose; can easily be moved to a sudden tear, or surprised into a broad laugh; but he loathes sentiment and has no turn for light pleasantry. He is a boon companion if you allow him to have his humor, and to talk about himself; and he will stand by a friend in a quarrel, with life and purse, however soundly he may be cudgeled.

John Bull is well intentioned and not particularly quick-witted, yet full of common sense. Unlike America's Uncle Sam, he is not a figure of authority but a man of the soil, a farmer. Calling your pub the Bull sent a very clear message to its customers (many of whom probably looked and behaved just like the national figurehead) that this was a proper English pub at its unchallenging and comfortable best, and you could expect warm beer and amiable chitchat with your fellow drinkers.

On the subject of the kind of topic that might be discussed at the Bull, the pub name in fact provides the origin of the common expression for an extremely tall tale. A 'cock and bull' story is likely to be untrue and with no real evidence to support it. The most likely source for this phrase comes from two pubs located in the same town.

Stoney Stratford, now part of Milton Keynes, is located almost exactly halfway between London and Birmingham, and Oxford and Cambridge respectively. During the great coaching era of the late eighteenth and early nineteenth centuries, the town was an important stopover point for travellers. The two main coaching inns were THE COCK and the Bull and, because of the centrality of their location, became known throughout the country as a hub of news and information. Not that the information was always reliable, however: according to local hearsay, a piece of information discussed at one pub had changed almost unrecognizably by the time it was retold at the second pub, a mere fifteen minutes away, as a result of which many items of news were dismissed as 'Cock and Bull' tales.

Rumour has it the entire government are going to relaunch their careers after the next general election, when their current ones will almost certainly be over, by forming a new chain of pub and restaurants called simply the Cock and Bull.

The Bush
THE MOST ANCIENT SYMBOL FOR AN ALEHOUSE

There are two theories behind this name, both dating back hundreds of years. The first comes from the earliest days of pubs. In Anglo Saxon times the village alehouse was just a normal house; the ale wife showed that she had ale available for drinking by fixing a green bush from the roof. That may also be where the popular pub name **The Holly Bush** comes from as they grabbed any bush to hand, the greener and tougher the better. This bit of early advertising was a precursor of the pub sign.

The second name actually derives more from a tree than a bush – the chequer (or chequers) tree, once common throughout Europe but now found only in ancient woodlands around Britain. It is thought that the tree is so called because its bark peels off in roughly rectangular pieces, giving it the appearance of a chequerboard. During the boom in beer drinking (and making) of the early Middle Ages and before the introduction of hops (see THE WHEATSHEAF), chequer berries were added to beer (or 'ale', as it was known) to flavour it and were widely used by brewers all over Britain. Many of those who brewed their own ale had their own chequer trees to supply them with fruit and so called their taverns after the tree. This is why some of the oldest pubs in Britain are still called THE CHEQUERS (see that entry for a different origin of the name), **Chequer Tree**, **Chequer Bush** or the Bush, and why the ancient symbol for an alehouse is a bush.

The California Arms
(Belmont, Surrey)

WAS THERE EVER A GOLD RUSH IN SURREY?

In 1850 John Gibbons was caught poaching a pheasant on the Northey estate in Cheam, Surrey. At that time, many poor families only survived by poaching. It was very risky, however: the hand of the law fell heavily upon transgressors. Being caught stealing in this way meant at best several years in prison, at worst being hanged. Not wishing to take any chances, Gibbons, grandson of the landlady at the Little Hell Alehouse on the Brighton Road (so named because of its popular, but illegal, gambling den deep in the cellar), fled to California, then in the throes of the Gold Rush.

Too sensible to risk everything again by panning for gold, Gibbons made his fortune running a supply store for the gold prospectors and returned to his home village of Belmont in 1860 where he built a public house, calling it the California Arms in honour of the part of America stolen from the Mexicans when gold was first found in their hills and rivers.

He might also have been hinting about the powerful appeal of his golden beer . . . If he was, it worked and a mini beer-rush happened as the fame of Gibbons's pub spread throughout the area. Thanks to the pub, there are still many references to California, with several buildings and other landmarks bearing the name locally. Even the railway station was originally called after this western US state.

In 1941 the California Arms was badly damaged during a German air raid, an event marked by the bravery of a British soldier, Private Gibb, who held up the crumbling roof for three hours while a woman trapped in the wreckage was rescued. Gibb was subsequently awarded the British Empire Medal for his heroism. The California Arms was then rebuilt in 1955, although it is now known, more prosaically, as the Belmont Country Carvery.

The Captain Kidd
(Wapping, London)

THE INFAMOUS PIRATE WHO FAILED TO PROVE HIS INNOCENCE

As any schoolboy will confirm, Captain Kidd (1645–1701) was a notorious pirate. Unfortunately for him, the good captain didn't see himself as a pirate at all. At fifty years of age, William Kidd was a respected English sea captain with an unblemished record. His reliability was the reason the British government invited him to lead a privateering expedition in 1695. At this time ships of those nations England was at war with were regarded as fair game and a privateer was permitted to attack them and loot their cargo. When Kidd sailed, he knew England was once again at war with France and therefore had carte blanche to steal the cargo of any French ship. Kidd was also taxed with attacking any pirates he came across.

Kidd had various backers who had invested in his ship and crew and they wanted results and a large cut of his winnings, so he was under real pressure to produce results. Consequently he did cut the odd corner but remained firmly on the privateering side of piracy. As his small fleet patrolled the entrance to the Red Sea, he sighted two Armenian vessels sailing under French passes and duly intercepted them, as he was legally entitled to do. But the ships' owners protested to the English authorities and Kidd was amazed to find himself arrested and branded a pirate when he later docked in New York. Kidd protested his innocence and forwarded the French passes to the correct authorities in England, fully expecting to be exonerated when he returned

proved to be his loudest denouncers, terrified of being impli-
cated in piracy. During the two years before his case was
heard, the French passes that proved his innocence mysteriously disappeared (they have recently been rediscovered)
and so he was convicted. Kidd was hanged on 23 May 1701
at Execution Dock in Wapping, close to the riverside pub
that now bears his name. His body was gibbeted – left to
hang in an iron cage over the Thames for twenty years –
making possibly the world's most macabre pub sign. It
makes it all the more harrowing that history's most famous
pirate was, in fact, an innocent man, a victim of behind-the-
scenes skulduggery and the old boys' network.

The Case is Altered

A LEGAL EXPRESSION OR A SPANISH STRIP CLUB?

There are several pubs in England going by this name, or,
with the addition of a single letter, the **Cause is Altered**, and
drinkers have often debated, long into the night, the origins
of possibly the most unusual pub name in English history.
Unsurprisingly, there are several theories, each depending
on the individual pub. One suggestion, involving the Case
is Altered in Bentley, near Ipswich, is that the first landlady
had been famously easygoing about the payment of bar
bills, until she married, that is, and her new husband took
a rather different view, soon altering the situation.

In Dover, the Cause is Altered is thought to have been
named to indicate to foreign travellers that England was
no longer a Catholic country. Another theory stems from
the time when farmers and herdsmen would stop at the

inn on the way to market, the pub's name a corrupted version of a local expression, 'the cows are halted'. In Banbury what was the Weavers Arms became the Case is Altered, the pub sign depicting a barrister interrogating a local man in the courthouse, after the company of weavers supposedly won an important legal case there.

Another theory, this time based on a pub in Harrow, suggests a phrase imported from Spain during the Peninsular War (1807–14). British soldiers taking a rest from the fighting would have been entertained at a 'house of dancing' (possibly an early type of strip club), or, in Spanish, *casa de saltar*, which could have become corrupted over time to 'case is altered'. But a far more likely origin of the phrase, and hence the pub name, can be traced to one Edmund Plowden (1518–85), a celebrated lawyer and theorist of the Tudor period.

A committed Catholic, Plowden was appointed a Member of the Council of Marches soon after the Catholic Queen Mary ascended to the throne in 1553 and began persecuting the Protestants. However, within a few years Mary had died and her half-sister Elizabeth became queen. She soon set about re-establishing the Protestant faith and Plowden's once meteoric career predictably faltered.

The new queen did offer to promote Plowden to the position of Lord Chancellor, the second highest office in the land, but this was on the condition he adopted the Anglican faith. Plowden declined but such was the eloquence of his defence of his faith that, instead of throwing him into the Tower of London and cutting off his head, the common fate of opponents to the crown, Elizabeth retained him as a legal adviser. As a result, Catholics in trouble were soon queuing up at Plowden's chambers seeking legal

Plowden's most famous case was representing a prominent Catholic who stood accused of hearing Mass. The accusations against the defendant had not been denied but as the trial wore on it dawned on Plowden that Mass had been held, in this instance, for the sole purpose of revealing to the Protestant authorities those who had attended and had therefore been conducted by a layman, not a priest. It was entrapment. Realizing this, Plowden immediately halted proceedings with this simple statement: 'No priest, no Mass. The case is altered.'

The expression soon became standard legal terminology and was brought into even wider use by BEN JONSON when he wrote a comedy called *The Case is Altered* (*c*.1597), which proved very popular. It is thought that some canny innkeepers then chose the unusual expression as the name of their pub to make it stand out all the more from the local competition. It obviously worked as hundreds of years later not only are those pubs still going strong but their names haven't altered.

The Cat And Cabbage
(Rotherham, Yorkshire)

TIGER AND ROSE BY ANOTHER NAME

At first glance this may appear to be another of those ridiculous theme names, but nothing could be further from the truth. The Cat and Cabbage is actually an army pub and its name relates to this.

In 1881 the York and Lancashire Regiment was formed

by uniting two other regiments, the York and Lancasters and the Yorkshire North Ridings. The new regiment, whose main recruiting area was south Yorkshire, particularly around the town of Rotherham, fought with distinction during many major conflicts, including the Boer War, the two world wars and the Suez Crisis of 1956.

Soon after Suez, in 1958, the 1st Battalion was disbanded and they finally gave up their regimental badge in 1968. The cap badge of the York and Lancasters was quite distinctive, consisting as it did of a tiger and a cabbage rose – the rose for Yorkshire and the tiger representing their predecessors' action in India – and this had led to the soldiers becoming known throughout the world by the fond nickname of the Cat and Cabbages.

The Cat and Fiddle

ENGLAND'S TRUE QUEEN OR THE MURDERER OF THE PRINCES?

Cat and Fiddle

There are many Cat and Fiddle public houses around Britain and opinion is divided on the origin of their unusual name. Discounting a tall tale of a violin-playing pub cat (although there probably is such a story somewhere), there are several theories. One suggests it could derive from *chat fidèle* (French for 'faithful cat'), the phrase having become corrupted over time. By contrast, *Brewer's Dictionary of Phrase and Fable* suggests that Caton le Fidèle, referring to a former Governor of Calais (at the time an English colony in France), may be the source of the name. According to this theory, although not supported by any evidence, one of Caton's soldiers retired to England and opened a tavern named after his old master, but the English had trouble pronouncing the name and so he changed it to Cat and Fiddle.

Another possibility is that the name is a mangling of Catherine la Fidèle – Catherine the Faithful – a nickname for Catherine of Aragon (1485–1536). Catherine's story is an unfortunate one. Aged fifteen, the Spanish princess was married to Arthur, eldest son of Henry VII, who was so desperate to cement relations between England and Spain that when Arthur died of a fever a few months later, he promptly re-betrothed Catherine to his surviving son, Henry, then only eleven. Poor Catherine then had to wait for eight years under virtual house arrest for her second wedding.

Despite its less than romantic start, the marriage of Henry VIII and Catherine of Aragon was initially a very happy one. Both were highly educated, talented rulers in a partnership of equals: when he went to France on a military campaign, Henry appointed her regent. And when the Scots invaded, she inspired the English army to victory at Flodden. The young king had loveknots with their entwined initials carved into all their palaces.

The trouble set in with Catherine's difficulty in producing a male heir. She fell pregnant six times but none of her children lived longer than fifty-two days. In 1516 she finally gave birth to a healthy girl, Mary. Henry, however, still considered a male heir essential. The Tudor dynasty was new (he was only the second king) and its legitimacy might still be tested. A long civil war (1135–54) had been fought the last time a woman (Henry I's daughter, Mathilda) had inherited the throne.

But Catherine was no longer able to undergo further pregnancies, and Henry began to believe that his marriage was cursed. Finding confirmation of this in the Bible, which stated that if a man marries his brother's wife, the couple will be childless, he started looking around for someone else who might give him the son he needed. Unfortunately for Catherine, his eye fell on Anne Boleyn, a very ambitious maid of honour, who held out for marriage before the king could test out her son-bearing capabilities.

Catherine indignantly refused when it was suggested that she retire to a convent, and Henry's various appeals to the Pope to have their twenty-year marriage annulled were rejected. Henry blamed Catherine for this and punished her. In 1531 she was banished from court and her old rooms were given to Anne Boleyn. When Catherine's death was announced in 1536, Henry dressed in yellow to celebrate the news.

Many were shocked and angered by the king's harsh treatment of their much loved queen and this was only heightened by Henry's rejection of the Catholic Church to divorce her. To all staunch Catholics, Catherine la Fidèle remained England's true queen and it is argued that the choice of the name Cat and Fiddle for a pub was a coded message on behalf of the landlord for support for her and her religion, and hence a dangerous rejection of the king. (See also THE BULL.)

The fourth and most convincing theory – despite at least one Cat and Fiddle insisting that it was named after yet another Catherine, its former owner (no doubt a violin player too) – comes from one of our most popular nursery rhymes:

> Hey diddle diddle,
> The cat and the fiddle,
> The cow jumped over the moon;
> The little dog laughed to see such fun,
> And the dish ran away with the spoon.

Often regarded as one of the best-known nonsense poems of all time, there have been some interesting attempts to explain what inspired the rhyme. It turns out to be just as dangerous and subversive a story as that of Catherine la Fidèle.

'Hey Diddle Diddle', it is suggested, offers a cryptic commentary on Richard III's crooked path to the English throne. In April 1483, following the death of his brother Edward IV, Richard took over as regent on behalf of his thirteen-year-old nephew, Edward V. He then placed the young king and his even younger brother in the Tower of London, supposedly for their own safety. However, within weeks both boys had been declared illegitimate by an Act of Parliament, after which the 'Princes in the Tower' mysteriously disappeared.

Richard was then declared King of England on 6 July 1483.

People were inevitably suspicious, but it was far too dangerous to openly question the actions of the new king. Instead, the rhyme allowed their suspicions to be voiced but in a way that didn't directly point a finger at the culprits – using nonsense verse. Sir William Catesby (1450–85), a supporter of Richard who had helped him gain the throne, and who quickly rose to power as a result, was known publicly as the 'Catte'. It was whispered that the Cat had thought up the 'Fiddle' that had made Richard king: namely, the murder of his two nephews.

The Chequers
A CHEQUERED HISTORY?

The chequerboard as a pub sign goes back many years; indeed, it has been found by archaeologists on houses uncovered in Pompeii, suggesting that it was probably advertising a game like draughts or, as the Americans call it, checkers. It is not unusual to see customers having a quiet game of draughts or chess in a modern pub, of course, but the chequerboard hanging outside has a slightly different origin.

The Chequers Inn in Oxford, located on the site of an ancient monastery, is one of the oldest pubs in the city. Records indicate that during the fifteenth century the pub courtyard was shared with the house of a moneylender. At the time the symbol of a moneylender was a chequerboard, believed to have its origins in the easily portable checked cloth used by Romans to make their calculations. This set-up would have been mirrored in inns across the land – indeed the landlord of a pub might himself have been the moneylender – and appears to be the reason why so many establishments called the Chequers used the sign of a chequerboard: to show drinkers that the pub also provided banking services.

It is certainly true that in the Middle Ages innkeepers were known for practising other trades in addition to serving drinks: a bread-making publican might work from the **Baker's Arms,** for instance, and a brick-laying one from the **Bricklayer's Inn** – which accounts for the number of pubs and hotels with a trade-based name. Landlords were also well respected and trusted for their financial dealings, some even being depended upon by parish authorities to distribute doles for the poor and starving, and an 'exchequer board' would usually be displayed at these inns.

The word 'exchequer', referring to a treasury or financial institution, goes back to the Middle Ages too. The *Dialogue Concerning the Exchequer* or *Dialogus de Scaccario*, written by Richard Fitzneal (c.1130–98), treasurer to Henry II, was a thesis on the overall practice of the English Exchequer, indicating the term was well established by that date. The word itself evolved from Old French, *eschequier*, which in turn comes from the medieval Latin word *scaccarium*, meaning 'chessboard' or 'chequerboard' and harking back again to the Romans and their portable calculators, not to mention those prototype pubs buried under volcanic ash in Pompeii.

Incidentally, Chequers, the house used by British prime ministers as a country retreat, probably acquired its name from its original owner, Elias Ostiarius – 'Ostiarius' or 'de Scaccario' (another version of the name), meaning an usher at the court of the Exchequer – whose coat of arms incorporated a chequerboard. According to another theory, however, the house is in fact called after the chequer trees growing in its grounds (see THE BUSH for a different interpretation of Chequers as a pub name). Arthur Lee, the last private owner of the place, recognized after the First World War that, whereas previously only the landed gentry had held positions in government, a new type of politician was emerging, one without his own grand country residence in which to relax or entertain foreign dignitaries. Lee resolved this by handing over Chequers to the nation in 1921 to serve as a retreat for serving prime ministers. While we ordinary people have our Chequers in which to relax and entertain our acquaintances. I know which one of the two I'd rather spend an evening in.

The Childe Of Hale
(Hale, Cheshire)

A VERY TALL TALE?

The small village of Hale, on the River Mersey north of Liverpool, became one of the most celebrated villages in England in 1620, thanks to one of their local sons, John Middleton (1578–1623). As a child, Middleton became known simply as the Childe of Hale as he was such a tall boy and was recognized everywhere he went.

Local legend tells us that, aged twenty, Middleton drew the shape of a giant in the sand and lay down to sleep, wishing he could be the same size. And when he woke he found he was – at least that is what they say around those parts. What is recorded is that by the time John was twenty years old he had grown to nine foot three inches, which would have made him the tallest man most people would ever see, by some considerable margin: in the sixteenth century the average height of a man was only five foot six inches. Imagine the trouble he would have had with doorways, let alone ceilings. His cottage in Hale has two distinctive windows, side by side in the gable end, that locals claim their giant had to put his feet through each night in order to lie down and sleep. Local legend also mentions his great strength, which led the Sheriff of Lancaster, Gilbert Ireland, to employ him as a bodyguard. Hearing of this, James I, who had a fascination for both giants and dwarfs, invited both men to court.

In 1620 the king arranged a fight between his best wrestler and the Childe of Hale, which Middleton easily won, along with several other bouts, earning himself fame and respect at court. The king awarded Middleton £20, a princely sum in those days, and provided a splendid gown of gold, red and purple that a later portrait depicts Middleton wearing. Returning to Hale a hero, though sadly a penniless one as legend has it that his companions stole his money on the way home, Middleton settled down to live quietly in the village and was buried in the churchyard when he died in 1623. His epitaph reads: 'Here lyeth the bodie of John Middleton, the Childe of Hale. Nine feet three.' He is remembered today by that noblest of English honours – having a pub in his village named after him.

The Clog And Billycock
(Pleasington, near Blackburn, Lancashire)

THE LOCAL FOR THE SARTORIALLY CHALLENGED YOKEL

Originally this pub was called the **Bay Horse,** a common name for an inn. Bay is also the most common coloration for a horse, consisting as it does of a reddish-brown coat with a black mane and tail. But for thirty years the Bay Horse at Pleasington was known informally to locals as the Clog and Billycock after the eccentric yokel's outfit worn by Alfred Pomfret, its landlord: Pomfret always wore clogs, specially designed by his brother, and a billycock hat.

Clogs, a type of shoe traditionally made out of wood, have their origins in northern Europe, in Holland, Sweden, Denmark and Belgium. (Traditionally, Dutch children leave out a clog rather than a stocking at Christmas.) In England, when the Industrial Revolution was in full swing during the mid nineteenth century, factory and mill workers had need of footwear that was cheap, strong and easily available, and so the clog became popular, particularly in Lancashire, the shoe being worn from around 1835 until the end of the First World War. English clog dancing dates from this period, too, as workers would tap their wooden footwear on the floorboards in time to the shuttles flying across the looms in the cotton mills. Clog fighting was not uncommon, becoming the traditional way to settle disputes – two opponents would kick each other until one submitted, while their fellow workers placed bets on the outcome. Today clogs are still worn for protective reasons in some regions by workers in mines, farms or factories; otherwise they have virtually disappeared, apart from brief periods, such as the 1970s, when they come back into fashion and then clomp out again.

The billycock hat, resembling a bowler in shape, was one of the most common forms of titfer in Britain during the mid 1800s. It apparently takes its name from the nephew of the 1st Earl of Leicester, William (Billy) Coke, for whom it was originally made in 1850, although it is also claimed that it may have been Edward Coke, younger brother of the 2nd Earl of Leicester, who placed the first order for the hat. But if so, then why is it not known as a teddycock? Another theory is that the name may relate to the cocked shape a hat might take after its owner had been beaten by someone (a bully, by definition), and hence it is a corruption of 'bullycock'. (And no, I don't believe that story either.)

In 1849 the London hat-makers Thomas and William Bowler took an order from the firm of hatters Locke & Co. to produce a tight-fitting, low-crowned, strong hat to protect gamekeepers from being hit on the head by branches or angry poachers. When Mr Coke, probably William, arrived to collect the hats, he is said to have placed one on the floor and jumped on it to test its strength. Confident that it could hold his weight, he paid the bill and the billycock hat went into production. Somewhat modified, it later became known as the bowler hat after the two men who originally designed it.

The Coach and Horses

CAN DRINKING AND DRIVING LEAVE YOU HEADLESS?

The Coach and Horses is one of the best-known British pub names. For many centuries, prior to the invention of the railway, the only form of transport around towns and cities, and indeed between them, was by horse. Or, for the well-off, by horse and carriage. In many cities, especially in London, hackney carriages (consisting of a horse and carriage and licensed for hire since 1662) became an essential part of life, whisking city folk about their business day and night, before they were supplanted by the HANSOM CAB. Between the cities larger stagecoaches, pulled by four or more horses, carried travellers across the land. These journeys took days and pubs prospered along the most popular routes, providing food and lodging to the weary travellers passing through (see also THE BULL). The innkeeper would advertise this with a sign depicting both a coach and a horse, indicating that not only did the place have everything the passengers could wish for, it also had stables so that the sweating mounts could be fed and rested, although probably out of sight and round in the back yard. In London, where there are still over fifty Coach and Horses pubs, these establishments were obviously popular with the many hackney carriage drivers, who could only take their breaks at a tavern catering for both man and horse, and accounting for why the name is so widespread across the capital. Indeed it is easy to imagine a carriage driver arriving in an unfamiliar district and asking another driver for the nearest Coach and Horses.

Not content with this rather prosaic explanation of the

have been known to regale their customers with a rather
different story, however. It goes something like this:

One dark and lonely night, as the wind swept relentlessly
across the moors, I was driving home after working the
late shift. Looking forward to a warm bed, snuggled up
to my wife, I'd been driving for about half an hour and
hadn't seen another car. But as I slowed down to round
the last bend before the moorland became forest, I saw
something so terrifying I don't think I can ever drive
along that stretch of road again. For there, right in front
of me and charging at full speed, was a coach, straight
out of the eighteenth century, pulled along by four galloping horses. There was a ghostly blue haze around the
whole image but it seemed real enough and, as the coach
came closer, I jammed on the brakes, stalling the engine.
With the horses now bearing down upon me, I frantically
tried to restart the car, but at the last minute the coach
swerved to one side and thundered past. As it swept by, I
caught sight of the driver, lashing furiously with his whip
– he appeared to have no head at all. The passengers were
staring through the windows as the coach raced by. I can
still see their skull-like faces. The crashing of the hooves
soon disappeared behind me as the coach and horses galloped away across the moors. I finally managed to start
the car and drove home as fast as I could.

This story is told in various forms all over Britain. Sometimes the coach is pulling into the driveway of an old manor
house and at other times it is stationary, parked outside an
inn that was later renamed the Coach and Horses.

The most famous Coach and Horses, and one of my favourite pubs even though there is no ghost story attached, is in Greek Street, Soho. Chiefly famous for being the haunt of Jeffrey Bernard, it was used as the setting for Keith Waterhouse's play *Jeffrey Bernard is Unwell*. Bernard, who died in 1997, was a well-known journalist and columnist, notable for his hilarious 'Low Life' contribution for the *Spectator* magazine. He was also a notorious drinker and could be found in his usual seat at the end of the bar in the Coach and Horses arguing with its landlord, Norman Balon. Both are featured in the play that takes its title from the notice frequently posted by *Spectator* editors to explain why the writer's column was missing that particular week, 'unwell' being an easily seen through euphemism for 'incapacitated due to drink'. But Bernard was usually forgiven, such was the popularity of his work during what was a golden period of British journalism.

Bernard fondly described Balon as 'London's rudest landlord', and his witticisms and anecdotal stories were regularly documented by the writer, which, in turn, led to a degree of fame for the publican and an autobiography, published in 1991 and entitled *You're Barred, You Bastards*. Londoners and tourists alike would beat a path to the Coach and Horses just to experience Balon's version of hospitality, or in the hope that Bernard himself might be at the bar. (for other Soho pubs see also THE FRENCH HOUSE and THE JOHN SNOW.)

The Cock

LANDLORD, THERE'S A CHICKEN IN MY BEER!

The name of this pub, found in varying forms across Britain – the **Cock Inn, Cock Tavern, Cock and Bottle, Cock and Trumpet** and **Cock and Pie** – largely derives from that less than delightful old English pastime: cockfighting. Until it was banned in 1835 in England and Wales and all British territories overseas (the Scots took another sixty years to follow suit), men would train their cockerels to fight and take them to pubs to compete with other birds. Although cockerels naturally fight each other over food and mating rights – the source of the expression 'the pecking order' – such skirmishes are usually over in seconds. In the 'cockpit', however, roosters were encouraged to fight for up to half an hour at a time while money was won and lost on the outcome. Usually at least one of the birds would be killed and even the eventual winner could be torn to shreds in the process, dying soon afterwards.

A number of expressions from cockfighting still pepper the English language. 'Battle royal' is good example, applied these days to a zealously fought contest, sporting or otherwise, one that might be waged on the football pitch, in the boardroom or between warring factions of any kind and on any battlefield, literal or metaphorical. The expression entered the English language during the 1670s via the obsession at that time with cockfighting. It was such a popular pastime that people of every class, even the aristocracy and members of the royal family, would send their prized birds into the fray. The royal cockerels were usually the most magnificent of all and consequently often the best fighting birds. Cockfighting would take place in stages. In the first instance, sixteen birds would be dropped into a pit and allowed to fight each other randomly – usually they would scrap with the nearest bird – until eight of them had been pecked to pieces and were unable to continue. The surviving eight would then be sent into battle again for round two, until only four remained, and so on until the two most resilient cockerels fought in the final. By that time, even the champion cockerels were beginning to wilt but, spurred on by their owners and the shouts of the crowd, they would fight to the death. It was the royal cockerels that engaged in the fiercest, and subsequently most talked-about, fights. They truly were battle royals.

It is equally possible that some pubs acquired their name thanks to a recipe that was popular throughout England in the sixteenth century. Cock ale was a type of beer flavoured with spices and chicken. To make the ale, innkeepers would take ten gallons of beer and add five pounds of raisins, some cloves and other spices. Then they prepared a cockerel, the older the better, by hitting it with a stone until it was completely flat. The cock was then boiled in the mixture, which was left to stand for nine days, when the cock would be removed, the ale now ready for bottling. I think I need to take a break here . . .

How the **Cock and Trumpet** got its name has a far less eye-watering history, which can be traced to the Elizabethan poets, who would associate the crowing cock with a trumpet player. A good example can be found in Shakespeare's *Hamlet* (Act 1, Scene 1):

> . . . I have heard,
> The cock that is the trumpet to the morn,
> Doth with his lofty and shrill sounding throat
> Awake the god of the day . . .

More straightforwardly, the **Cock and Bottle** derives from a sign used to advertise a tavern selling both bottled and barrelled beer. The 'cock', in this case, being the peg of the barrel from which the ale was drawn. (For the origin of the expression 'cock and bull story', based on a pub called the Cock, see THE BULL.)

The Crooked Billet
I HEARD IT WAS THE GRAPEVINE

The Romans used to display a bunch of grapes outside a wine house to indicate the grapes had been harvested and the new wine would be flowing. A crooked billet literally means a bent or crooked stick or other piece of wood shaped like a shepherd's 'crook'. As a pub name, it may well have evolved from the image of the grapevine after it had been stripped clean of its fruit by birds within minutes of being displayed outside the tavern. There is no real evidence to indicate that the empty grapevine is the basis for the pub name, but it's a good story. As is the idea of an old country pub having its sign blown away in a gale, leaving a rudimentary wooden pole, probably not straight, standing outside the inn, causing locals to nickname it the Crooked Billet. In truth, nobody really knows why pubs are called this other than that a crooked billet is a bent stick of some kind.

Another meaning of 'billet', of course, is a lodging for soldiers. One establishment in Stoke Row near Henley on Thames, called the Crooked Billet since it was built in 1642, claims to have provided lodging (albeit in secret) for a rather less upright citizen (definitely 'crooked', in this case). This was none other than the notorious highwayman Dick Turpin (1705–39), purported to have had a love affair with the landlord's daughter Bess. Although there is no evidence Turpin ever had a lover called Bess, he did have a horse by the same name, stolen from a Mr Major at the point of a flintlock pistol. Black Bess, as the highwayman named his new charge, was the fine thoroughbred that would eventually lead to Turpin's capture. Furious at the loss of his beloved horse, Major handed notices around the pubs of London, describing both the horse and highwayman, and offering a substantial reward for its return. Magnificent and distinctive in appearance, Bess was soon traced to the THE RED LION in Whitechapel, where the outlaw had stabled it and Turpin's accomplice was arrested when he returned to collect Black Bess, eventually leading to the capture of the highwayman himself.

The Cross Keys
DRINKERS' HEAVEN?

Any public house bearing this name would have had, at one time, strong religious connections, and the symbol of the cross keys is still closely associated with Christianity. The New Testament tells the story of a young fisherman who became one of the twelve disciples and whom Jesus renamed Peter, from the Greek word *petros*, meaning 'rock', because he was to become the rock upon which 'I build my church' and to whom one day he would give 'the keys to the kingdom of heaven' (Matthew 16: 18–19).

After his death, Jesus's supporters wandered around in their long robes and sandals, gathering more followers along the way, until the Romans tired of what they perceived as their disruptive influence and crucified most of them. As Jesus had predicted, Peter was their leader and, according to Catholic tradition, became the first Pope. The crossed keys are his symbol, perhaps also in oblique reference to the manner of his death – by crucifixion. At his own request, he was crucified upside down because he felt he was not worthy to die in the same manner as Jesus. Traditionally, St Peter is the guardian of heaven and the keys unlock its gate – indeed paintings of him often show him holding the keys. To this day, the Pope wears the Fisherman's Ring – a signet ring showing Peter fishing from a boat and used for sealing official documents – and displays the symbol of the cross keys in honour of St Peter.

Over the last two thousand years, the sign of St Peter's crossed keys has been displayed over taverns, hostels, hotels and even private houses advertising board and lodgings to the weary traveller or pilgrim. There's also a bit of a joke behind the use of this symbol as a pub sign for everyone who thinks that a good pub is, well, heaven. And so now, when you next hear any joke that starts along the lines of: 'An Englishmen, Scotsman and Irishman all knocked on the pearly gates of heaven and St Peter said . . .' you'll know that's the very St Peter who has the keys to heaven, and who inspired the symbol of the crossed keys, used since the dawn of Christianity.

The Crown and Arrows

A SAINTLY ROYAL TARGET

St George was not the first patron saint of England. Hundreds of years before we adopted the Libyan hero (see

The Crown and Arrows

there was actually a Anglo-Saxon king who held that distinction: St Edmund the Martyr, King of East Anglia (841–69). Edmund, who is thought to have descended from previous East Anglian monarchs, was crowned king, aged just fifteen, on Christmas Day in 855.

It was a turbulent time in English history. The Vikings, who had been raiding the eastern coastline since 800, began settling in East Anglia in 865, around ten years into the young king's reign. Until then, Edmund had been a peacefully minding his own business. A considerate ruler, he treated his subjects with respect and favour. He also immersed himself in the Christian religion, once even spending an entire year in prayer in his royal tower at Hunstanton.

While this was good for the soul, it wasn't so good at discouraging marauding Vikings and in early 869 two Viking chiefs, Hubba and Hinguar, invaded King Edmund's domain. Edmund fought back fiercely and repelled the invading army, re-establishing peace in East Anglia. Unfortunately for the young king, the Danes returned in larger numbers later in the year, this time led by the wonderfully named Ivor the Boneless and his brother Ubbe Ragnarsson. One version of the events that followed suggests Edmund engaged them in battle at Hoxne, although another, more likely, story insists that Edmund, realizing his men were hopelessly outnumbered and reluctant to see any further slaughter, disbanded his army and rode away. He was soon caught by the Vikings, however, who demanded he accept them as his overlords and renounce the Christian faith, but the king refused. Even after torture Edmund declared his faith to be more important than his own life, so he was tied to a tree in front of the

Viking leader Hinguar. Once again, Edmund refused to renounce his faith and so Hinguar ordered his archers to use the king for target practice.

The story of the king's death and martyrdom was recorded a century later by his biographer, Abbo of Fleury, who was told it by St Dunstan, who in turn claimed to have heard it directly from one of Edmund's military commanders who had witnessed the whole thing. The *Anglo-Saxon Chronicle* tells it like this:

> The heathens then became brutally angry because he called on Christ to help him. They shot then with arrows, as if to amuse themselves, until he was all covered with their missiles as with bristles of a hedgehog, just as Saint Sebastian was. Then Hinguar, the dishonourable Viking, saw that the noble king still did not desire to renounce Christ and with resolute faith still called to him. Hinguar then commanded to behead the king and the heathens thus did. While this was happening, Edmund still called to Christ. Then the heathens dragged the holy man to slaughter, and with a stroke struck the head from him.

According to the legend, the Vikings tried to hide Edmund's severed head in a wood, but it called out and was rescued. His final resting place is the town of St Edmundsbury in Suffolk, otherwise known as Bury St Edmunds, which became famous during the final century of the first millennium because of the miracles reputedly performed at King Edmund's graveside.

In the same way that many pubs have been named in honour of our current patron saint, so St Edmund would have inspired landlords to use his name and image on their inn signs. While there is no Crown and Arrows pub at Bury St Edmunds (although the town does have a ROSE AND CROWN), a pub by that name can be found by St Edmund's Church at Shelton Lock, near Derby.

The Davy Lamp
EARLY EARLY-WARNING SYSTEM

The eldest of five children, Humphry Davy was born in Penzance, Cornwall, on 17 December 1778. A brilliant scientist, later fellow of the Royal Society and professor of the Royal Institution, Davy became hugely popular with the public and his lecture tours and experiments were always well attended, possibly because they were so dangerous – in 1812 laboratory accidents cost him two fingers and the use of one eye.

In 1814 Sir Humphry Davy (he had been knighted two years previously) settled back into his laboratory and, inspired by the Felling mine disaster of 1812, at a colliery near Newcastle, began work to improve the underground pit lighting and safety of miners. By 1815 he had produced a safety lamp that enabled miners to work deep seams despite the presence of methane or other flammable gases. At the time, all mines were illuminated by the naked flame and explosions were a constant hazard. But Davy discovered that a flame enclosed by a fine wire mesh could not ignite any dangerous gases (known as 'firedamp') as air could pass through the gauze, keeping the flame alight, but the holes in the mesh were too fine to allow the flame to pass the other way and ignite the firedamp. In addition, the flame inside the safety lamp would burn with a blue tinge if any firedamp were present. Placed near the ground, the lamp could also be used to detect denser gases, such as carbon monoxide, the invisible killer. If there was insufficient oxygen in the air, the flame would go out, acting as an early warning for miners to evacuate. No doubt canary lovers the world over were just as pleased as the miners by Davy's innovative ideas. (A canary in a cage had previously provided the early-warning system – a dead bird indicating the presence of toxic gases.)

Despite his many other significant scientific discoveries, it is the miner's safety lamp, and his contribution to the welfare of the men who worked the mines, that Davy is best remembered for, and to this day pubs in former mining communities all over Britain still bear the name of his life-saving invention.

The Dog Watch
THE NAVAL SHIFT SYSTEM AND ITS ARTFUL 'DODGE' WATCH

The Dog Watch, as a pub name, doesn't relate to dogs (see THE OLD DOG AND DUCK for those that do) but is an old nautical term still in regular use by modern sailors. The Royal Navy's peacetime watch system was first developed during the seventeenth century and has worked so efficiently for navies throughout the world there has never been any reason to modify it. At sea, it is vital for a ship to be manned twenty-four hours a day and there are three crucial areas that must never be left unattended: the bridge, the ship's control centre and the main communications office. To ensure there is sufficient manpower at all times, the working day of the crew is split into four-hour shifts, with the exception of the last watch or 'dog watch', which is split into two two-hour shifts.

Time	Name	Nickname
2000–0000	First watch	The first (Geoff Hurst)
0000–0400	Middle watch	Middle (Hey diddle diddle)
0400–0800	Morning watch	The morning
0800–1200	Forenoon watch	The forenoon
1200–1600	Afternoon watch	The afternoon
1600–1800	First dog watch	First dog
1800–2000	Last dog watch	Last dog
No specific time	All night in bed	All night in (Rin Tin Tin)

This makes seven watches in total, an odd number, which means that the schedule can be rotated to ensure the same team is not working the same shift every day. The dog watch has always been split into two so that all the sailors on the ship have a chance to have their evening meal. It is thought to be called the dog watch after being nicknamed the 'dodge watch' by early mariners. It is also possibly the origin of the expression 'dog tired'. Traditionally (presumably dating to the time when the watches didn't have watches) bells have been used to mark each half-hour of a watch, so that the sailors can tell how much time has elapsed; eight bells mark the end of a watch, except the first dog watch, of course, which finishes after four. Interestingly, the number of bells sounded at the last dog watch is 1-2-3-8 rather than 5-6-7-8, a tradition that goes back to 1797, when a group of mutineers planned to take over a ship at 'five bells in the dog watches', after which officers decreed that only one bell should be struck at 6.30 pm, instead of five.

The Dover Patrol

THE NAVAL COMMAND BEST REMEMBERED FOR A DARING WARTIME RAID

In June 1914 Britain entered the First World War. A major problem for any island nation in the time of war is the need to secure the seas, both to prevent invasion and to keep open supply lines. The Dover Patrol was set up to prevent enemy submarines using the Channel and it was soon to become one of the most important naval commands of the war.

From fairly modest beginnings, the Dover Patrol began to assemble a larger fleet, consisting of a wide range of craft, including mine sweepers, submarines, sea planes, aeroplanes, airships, destroyers and cruisers. These all began patrolling the North Sea and the English Channel, looking for German U-boats, laying mines and escorting merchant supply ships. They would engage the enemy, too, shelling its defences along the coast of Belgium and Holland. The Dover Patrol became so effective that German U-boats and warships were forced to sail from the south of England to the tip of Scotland to reach the open seas. Over the next four years of the Great War, the Dover Patrol managed to maintain vital supply routes, carry ground troops to the front lines and bring home the wounded while all the time encountering the deadly U-boats.

In April 1918 the patrol was involved in one of the most daring operations of the entire war. Back in 1905 the Belgians had built a large artificial harbour at Zeebrugge, and it was here that the occupying German navy had made a base for their U-boat fleet. On the morning of 23 April 1918, the Dover Patrol, under the command of Vice Admiral Sir Roger Keyes, attempted to eliminate the threat from the submarines by attacking Zeebrugge with the intention of blocking traffic in and out of the port by sinking three ships filled with concrete at the mouth of the Bruges Canal.

As the operation began, 200 Royal Marines went ashore to attack enemy guns defending the canal while the remaining 1,500 men of the fleet managed to sink two of the three ships across the lock gate, severely disrupting German naval operations.

On the British side, 200 men were killed and another 300 badly injured, but the raid was regarded as a major success for the troops involved and a key propaganda victory, with no less than eight Victoria Crosses being presented, the highest military award for valour. Each year, on St George's Day, the Battle of Zeebrugge is commemorated at the port and the men of the Dover Patrol remembered. As they are by any pub going by this name.

The Drunken Duck
(Ambleside, Cumbria)

A VERY RUDE AWAKENING ...

Many years ago an innkeeper's wife at the Station Hotel near Ambleside, in the heart of the Lake District, found a duck lying motionless on the cobblestones in the back yard. Saddened by the loss of the duck, but thinking how the bird would make a fine meal, she took it inside and plucked it ready for cooking. But the warmth of the fire restored the by now very bald duck back to indignant, quacking life. The landlord soon discovered the problem: a barrel had broken in the courtyard and beer had flooded the yard, pouring into the duck's feeding ditch. The duck had been not dead but dead drunk. Meanwhile, much to the delight of both locals and travellers alike, the landlady, full

The Drunken Duck

of remorse, knitted an outfit for the duck to keep it warm until some of its feathers grew back. When people started appearing from far and wide to see the pub's unusual pet, the canny landlord renamed the Station Hotel the 'Drunken Duck'. (For more on the use of 'duck' as a pub name, see THE OLD DOG AND DUCK.)

The Duke of Buckingham
RISE AND FALL OF 'THE HANDSOMEST-BODIED MAN IN ALL OF ENGLAND'

George Villiers was born on 28 August 1592, the son of a minor nobleman. When he was twelve years old, his father died, leaving George and his mother Mary in a vulnerable position as his elder half-brothers, offspring of his father's first marriage, were in control of the family estate. Hoping her good-looking son could become a success at court, Mary sent George to France so he could be trained in the gentlemanly arts of fencing, dancing and how to conduct himself at court.

All this paid off and in 1614, at the age of twenty-two, Villiers – described as the 'handsomest-bodied man in all of England' – had made his way into the court of King James I. The following year he was given the somewhat worrying title of Gentleman of the Bedchamber, and indeed rumour had it he and the king were more than just good friends. It certainly would explain why within another two years he had been made first an earl and then a marquess. Five years later, aged just thirty-one, Villiers became the 1st Duke of Buckingham – the highest-ranking subject outside the royal family – proving quite clearly that the king's bedchamber was the place to be for any aspiring career nobleman in the early seventeenth century.

Yet Villiers was also known for his partiality to the opposite sex. Indeed, the nursery rhyme 'Georgie Porgie' is said to mock him for this and in particular the way he abused his position, forcing any woman at court he fancied to sleep with him (he 'kissed the girls and made them cry'), which caused resentment all round. His luck finally ran out when he started switching his allegiance from the ageing king to his heir, Charles. The prince and duke, in disguise, set off on a mission to woo a Spanish princess (see THE ELEPHANT AND CASTLE).

The complete collapse of the negotiations was blamed on Buckingham's crass behaviour: to such an extent that the Spanish ambassador asked James to have him executed in Madrid. On his return, Buckingham tried to deflect this by insisting that war be declared on the Spanish. He then became embroiled in a series of disastrous military campaigns, including an attempt to repeat Drake's success in Cadiz (see THE GOLDEN HIND) which went wrong when his soldiers captured a wine warehouse and stopped to drink it dry, giving the Spanish the advantage.

When a furious House of Commons tried to punish Buckingham for his failures, James I simply dissolved Parliament. The final straw came when the former rent-boy-made-good accidentally lost over 4,000 men out of an army of 7,000 in the siege of St Martin de Ré. On his return to Portsmouth in August 1628, he was stabbed to death by John Felton, an army officer who had been wounded and was furious at his commander's lack of military judgement and at the loss of so many of his English comrades.

And so that was the end of the most famous Duke of Buckingham, hero to a few but sordid fool to many more. In Portsmouth, the place of his demise, a pub called the Duke of Buckingham commemorates him – one of many throughout the country.

Meanwhile the **Buckingham Arms** in Westminister is, rather aptly, not far from St James's Park. Any assocations with Buckingham Palace, right next to the park, must be quickly discounted, however. The Queen's residence was originally the home of a different gentleman entirely – John Sheffield, 1st Duke of Buckingham and Normandy – who built the house for his family in 1703. Sold to King George III in 1761 for the princely sum of £21,000, it was later to become the most famous royal palace in the world.

The Duke of York
NO ANGEL OF THE NORTH?

The city of Eboracum was founded in AD 71 as a military fort, or walled city, by the occupying Roman army. One hundred and fifty years later, Eboracum became the capital city of the BRITANNIA Inferior (Lower Britain – 'lower' in the sense of 'further away from Rome'), a subdivision of Britannia, in the north of the province. After the Romans finally left Britannia in 410, it became the turn of the Vikings to rampage across our island, murdering and pillaging everything in sight, and the city was renamed Jorvik by the invading armies. Eleven years later, Halfdan Ragnarsson conquered a large area of northern Britannia (mainly Yorkshire and Northumbria), and promptly declared himself the first King of Jorvik. But in 954, soon after the last king, Erik Bloodaxe, had been driven out of town, the native English re-established their control over the lands. In the process they anglicized its name to York – the capital of the north of England.

The title Duke of York was first created in the official Peerage of England for Edmund Langley, the fourth son of King Edward III. After the Wars of the Roses, in which York had fought Lancaster for the crown (see the THE ROSE AND CROWN), the title was then recreated as the title of the second son of the ruling monarch. The Dukes of York have been a pretty eccentric bunch, judging by the strong competition there is for which of them actually inspired the well-known nursery rhyme 'The Grand Old Duke of York' and pub names all over Britain.

My favourite contender for the duke behind the rhyme is Prince Frederick Augustus (1763–1827). In 1793 this Duke of York was appointed field marshal of the British army and given one simple brief, to invade France. But Frederick was never a great military leader and despite a minor victory over the French forces at Beaumont in April 1794, he failed to earn the trust and confidence of his men. This was compounded when his troops were hammered at Tourcoing in May and the duke was consequently relieved of his position. The hill he is supposed to have marched his men up and down in the rhyme, before having them accidently massacred, is thought to be Mont Cassell, in northern France, standing nearly six hundred feet above the Flanders coastal plain.

In the twentieth century there have been only three Dukes of York. The first was Queen Victoria's grandson George (1865–1936), who changed the royal surname from Saxe-Coburg and Gotha to Windsor when he became King

George V in 1910. As war with Germany was looming, this gave the royal family a desirably English air. The following Duke of York reluctantly became King George VI to save the day with the British people when Edward VIII scandalously abdicated in order to marry American divorcee Wallis Simpson against the wishes of either the royal family or Parliament. Prince Andrew, once notorious for a string of girlfriends with a colourful past, became the current Duke of York in 1986. But now all eyes are on the future Duke of York, Prince Harry, and how he will shape up.

The Duke's Head
THE UBIQUITOUS ARISTOCRAT

A generic title generally used by pubs that have changed their name more than once to honour whichever war hero was fashionable at the time. In Great Yarmouth the **Duke of Cumberland** became the **Duke of Clarence**, then the **Duke of Wellington** (see THE IRON DUKE) before settling on the name encompassing all dukes, and many pubs in England have done the same over the years.

Meanwhile, the **Duke Without a Head**, which used to stand at Wateringbury, near Maidstone in Kent before being demolished in 1990, acquired its name when the licence was transferred in 1940 from the old Duke's Head, located right next to it and now a private house. The local magistrate's order allowing the licence to be transferred stated: 'Permission is given to remove the Duke's Head', reading like a royal death warrant (see also THE KING'S HEAD). The humour in this was not lost on the new owners, who named their new establishment accordingly.

The Eagle and Child

BABIES DELIVERED BY BIRDS OF PREY? PULL THE OTHER ONE . . .

The Eagle and Child

The origin of this pub name can be traced to the fourteenth century. Sir Thomas Latham, who lived near to Lytham St Annes in Lancashire, had one legitimate child, Isabel. His wife failed to fall pregnant with his desired son and heir and, as so often the case with the great families of England, the maid soon fell pregnant instead and bore the healthy son her master wanted.

Desperate for a son to succeed him, Sir Thomas devised a plan to persuade his wife to adopt the boy as her own, legitimizing him in the process. He arranged for the child to be left at the base of a tree where he had recently observed eagles nesting. His plan was to claim the baby had been abandoned by the birds, a story that his wife apparently accepted, adopting the boy soon afterwards. But after Sir Thomas died it was his daughter, Isabel, who inherited the estate.

Locals were said to have commemorated this story of man's inability to really fool his wife by naming a local tavern the Eagle and Child, and several other establishments were similarly named in successive years across the country. The most famous inn by this name is in St Giles, Oxford, once the Royalist capital during the English Civil War (1641–51). It is claimed that the Chancellor of the Exchequer lodged there during the conflict and the building served as the paymaster's quarters for the Royalist army, their horses being fed and watered in the courtyard. The pub also has strong literary connections: C. S. Lewis (author of *The Lion, the Witch and the Wardrobe* and the rest of the Narnia books) and J. R. R. Tolkien (*The Hobbit* and *The Lord of the Rings*, both featuring child-sized hobbits being rescued by giant eagles) met at the Eagle and Child every Friday between 1939 and 1962 for drinks and conversation.

These days the pub is affectionately known by those wacky university students – destined to be running the nation's judiciary, industry and even government, God help us all – as the Bird and Bastard, the Bustard and Bastard, the Fowl and Foetus and, most ridiculous of all, the Bird and Brat. (For more on the symbol of the eagle in pub names, see THE SPREAD EAGLE.)

The Elephant and Castle

A SPANISH PRINCESS OR EMBLEM OF A WEAPON-MAKER TO THE KING?

The most common theory behind the origin of the Elephant and Castle is that it evolved from the name of Eleanor of Castile (1241–90), the much loved wife of Edward I. When she died outside Lincoln, the grief-stricken king erected a series of twelve crosses across the country, marking each place her body rested overnight on its final journey to Westminster Abbey. The final Eleanor Cross gave a new name to an area of London, Charing – a mangling of *Chère Reine*, 'Dear Queen' – Cross, so it's easy to see how her full name, Eleanor of Castile, might be thought to account for why another area of London, Elephant and Castle, is so called. Sadly, historians can trace no connection between her and south-east London.

Another theory runs that the name is a corruption of Infanta de Castile, the title traditionally given to the eldest daughter of the King of Castile. Some have argued that this was also Eleanor, but she was only one of a number of Spanish princesses associated with English royalty, including Catherine of Aragon (see THE CAT AND FIDDLE) and Maria, an infanta briefly and controversially engaged to Charles I in 1623. The young prince and his adviser (see THE DUKE OF BUCKINGHAM) travelled to Spain in disguise to try to arrange the marriage but things went so badly wrong that Charles returned to England brideless while Buckingham then tried to insist on war being declared against Spain. The rather cheeky argument ran that all Charles had really needed to do to find love was take the easier journey to south London and the much more welcoming arms of the Elephant and Castle.

Others have claimed the unusual name derives from a vision a man had on London Bridge in which he claimed to have seen an elephant with a castle on its back walking through the mist and clouds from the direction of the south. Although that sounds like something my granddad would have told me (he was from around that way), the story did become folklore in Newington during the seventeenth and eighteenth centuries.

But there is another, much more sensible reason. A record found in the Court Leet Book of the Manor of Walworth, a nearby London district, shows that on 21 March 1765 the council met at 'the Elephant and Castle in Newington'. The public house in question had been built on a site previously occupied by a smithy that had borne the same name and sign. The smithy had had connections with the Worshipful Company of Cutlers, whose coat of arms included an elephant with a castle (a howdah, or seat traditionally used by hunters in India) on its back.

Trading in knives, scissors and surgical instruments, the Worshipful Company of Cutlers is one of the livery companies of the City of London (see also THE GOAT AND COMPASSES and THE SWAN WITH TWO NECKS). On 4 December 1416 it received a royal charter from King Henry V in recognition of the weapons supplied for the Battle of AGINCOURT the previous year. The coat of arms was first granted to the company around 1476 and in 1622 this was modified to its current design. The crest includes two elephants (a reference to the Indian elephant ivory used as handles for knives and swords) and a shield decorated with three pairs of crossed swords (a reference to the demand for weapons most cutlers fulfilled). Standing proudly at the top of the crest is the famous elephant with its castle.

The Flying Bedstead
(Hucknall, Nottinghamshire)

BEDKNOBS AND JOYSTICKS

In 1953 Hucknall Aerodrome in Nottinghamshire was the home of research into the world's first vertical take-off and landing aircraft (VTOL) using engine thrust alone, unaided by wings and rotors. The Rolls-Royce Thrust-Measuring Rig (TMR) was the forerunner of the Lunar Landing Research Vehicle (LLRV). Developed in America for the Apollo Space programme, the LLRV was used by astronauts as part of their training for controlling the Lunar Module when descending to the surface of the moon, although the entire programme came under threat after Commander Neil Armstrong was nearly killed when his LLRV crashed during testing. Both VTOLs consisted of a simple platform with four legs, resembling a bed, and both were nicknamed the 'Flying Bedstead' during development.

In 1957 a test pilot, Air Commodore Larsen, also crashed during testing at Hucknall Aerodrome, resulting in a fatal accident. These early research and development flights are commemorated by the nearby pub, also called the Flying Bedstead.

The Flying Dutchman

THE GHOSTLY CAPTAIN AND HIS CREW CONDEMNED TO SAIL THE SEAS FOR EVER

There are many Flying Dutchman pubs throughout Britain and as many theories supporting the origin of the name. Steam-train enthusiasts will point to the legendary locomotive of the same name operating mainly along the London to Exeter route between 1849 and 1892, although, in fact, like many steam trains of the period, it was named after a famous racehorse. Bred in Yorkshire, the Flying Dutchman triumphed in every race he entered, bar one, including the Derby and the St Leger in 1849, the year the train was first launched. (If that's what you do with trains.) Both the locomotive and the racehorse may well have inspired a few inns and taverns to bear their name (see also 'Pubs Named in Honour of Famous Racehorses'). But the name itself goes back much further, to events alleged to have taken place four centuries ago, somewhere near the Cape of Good Hope at the tip of South Africa.

The most celebrated ghost ship the world has ever known takes its name from a Dutch captain, a man called Van Something or Other (opinions vary), who was famous for the speed at which he was able to travel between Holland and the Far East along the trade routes of the seventeenth century. Legend has it that on one return journey he ordered his crew to tackle the Cape of Good Hope in the teeth of a storm, instead of taking shelter in nearby False Bay. His crew, suspecting the belligerent captain to be more interested in his own reputation than the safety of his men, pleaded with the old seadog, but Captain van Cantankerous refused to change course. As he left the quarterdeck, he swore a blasphemous oath, challenging the might of God, and then attacked a man who had dared question his decision, running him through with his cutlass and throwing him overboard.

The moment the body hit the water, the dead sailor immediately reappeared on deck and Captain van Reckless drew his pistol, only for it to explode in his hand. The ghostly fellow now spoke: 'As a result of your actions you are now condemned to sail the oceans for eternity with a crew of dead men, bringing death to all who sight your spectral ship. You will never again make land or know a moment's peace.'

And ever since, the ghostly *Flying Dutchman* has been trying to sail around the Cape into the teeth of fierce winds, or leading other ships on to the rocks, condemning to death any sailor who lays eyes upon her and, strangely enough (according to those who lived to tell the tale), passing on letters addressed to people long dead.

There have been many supposed sightings of the ghost ship, including one by a young midshipman who later became King George V and who recorded, on 11 July 1881, exactly what he and the duty lookout had witnessed on that dark night: 'A strange red light, as of a phantom ship all aglow, in the midst of which light the mast, spars and sails of a brig two hundred yards distant stood out in strong relief.' And yes, apparently they did speak to each other like that in those days. Unfortunately for the lookout, he was to suffer the curse of the *Flying Dutchman* and fell to his death from the mast. As for the royal midshipman, well, he probably spent the rest of the night tucked up in his silk dressing gown and Indian cotton sheets, having his brow stroked by his butler.

Dozens of other sightings have been reported over the years, including one in 1939 by an entire beach full of people who described almost exactly the same thing. Despite not knowing their tall ships from their elbows, they could still describe in minute detail what they had apparently seen.

Another version of the legend tells of a different Dutch captain, also Captain van Something or Other, who rounded the Cape mulling over his idea of establishing a trading post in the area where Dutch trade ships could take on fresh water and other provisions (now known as Cape Town). So deep was he in thought that he failed to notice a big rock and sailed straight into it. As Captain van Shipwreck began to sink, he called out: 'I will round this cape even if I have to sail round it until doomsday.' Legend has it that whenever you look into the eye of the storm at the Cape you will see Captain van Perseverance still trying to sail around it. Now, I have stood at the Cape many, many times but I have never seen anything looking remotely like a tall ship, seventeenth-century or otherwise. I have seen a few pleasure cruisers that are so old they look like they might have been designed for Alfred the Great, but never the *Flying Dutchman*.

The final version of the *Flying Dutchman* legend (made into an opera by Richard Wagner in 1843) dates to 1680 or 1730, depending on who you believe. This tells of a Captain van Godfearing who insulted the devil who then condemned him to sail the oceans for ever, leaving him with one small glimmer of hope. Only through the love of a faithful woman can he be released from the curse. And so Captain van No Hope returns to the shore every seven years in search of a faithful woman. Well, good luck with that in Cape Town, captain.

The Foresters' Arms
A FRIENDLY SOCIETY IN NEED . . .

Now known as the Foresters Friendly Society, the Ancient Order of Foresters was officially formed in 1834. An even earlier version, the Court of the Ancient Order of Foresters, is acknowledged to have existed in England in 1790, though no official records were kept because mutual or friendly societies were outlawed in Britain at the time. Fearful of a French-style revolution of the working classes, the government had prohibited membership of all unions (see THE ODDFELLOWS' ARMS). The Foresters claim to have first evolved from the craft guilds of the Middle Ages, and that is quite possibly true but, like the Oddfellows and most other friendly societies, there are no records of membership or articles of association from that time to prove it.

It was after the Norman Conquest that the forests of England were first categorized. The earliest written reference comes from 1079 when William the Conqueror reserved an area of land in south Hampshire for royal hunting and called it the New Forest. Other royal forests still exist, including the Forest of Arden in Warwickshire and Sherwood Forest in Nottinghamshire (see THE ROBIN HOOD). Foresters were employed by the king to manage the royal land. They held a position in society similar to that of a local sheriff or law enforcer such as a magistrate. Responsible for patrolling the land and capturing poachers, their duties also included negotiating the sale of timber, one of the most widely used building materials of the time, and replanting stock. Criminals and bands of outlaws would hide in the forests and the forester's responsibilities extended to organizing gangs of armed men to hunt down such lawbreakers. This was dangerous as many confrontations ended in a fight to the death, but foresters could make a decent living out of their job, and they were usually well respected among the law-abiding.

While the medieval foresters probably did form their own friendly societies at the time of the guilds in the thirteenth century, it is not clear that these had any meaningful influence on the Ancient Order of Foresters when it formed in 1834. At their first meeting in Leeds, the members of the society declared support for their fellow men who fell into need 'as they walked through the forest of life', and insisted their duty was to support any family who became distressed when the major wage earner fell ill or was unable to work for any other reason. This charity became the major function of the Foresters, whose members initially paid a few pennies a week into a common fund from which sick pay, funeral costs and poverty grants could be drawn.

In 1813 its predecessor, the Royal Order of Foresters, expanded and had begun to establish subsidiary branches around the country. The venues of these meetings would soon become the pubs and hotels we now know as the **Foresters** or the Foresters' Arms. As with the Oddfellows, the principles of the Foresters would be incorporated into the trade unions representing workers later in the century. At the beginning of the twentieth century, the British government started applying the ideology of the friendly societies to the law of the land and a classless society began to draw nearer. (Well, here's hoping.)

These days the Foresters Friendly Society is a financial institution with no shareholders or any obvious influence from the City. Acting independently for the sole benefit of their members, who share in all profits earned, the organization has remained true to its original principles and has continued to provide charity for its members instead of dividends to greedy investors.

The French House
(Soho, London)

THE HEART OF THE FRENCH RESISTANCE IN THE HEART OF LONDON

The French House in Dean Street is one of the smallest pubs in London. Although not one of the oldest, it has one of the most vibrant histories of them all. During the 1950s the French House became the drinking den of choice for most of London's artistic community. Every day writers, artists, actors, musicians, singers and songwriters could be found holding court in the small downstairs bar, or hunched over a humble lunch in the cramped upstairs dining room, sharing stories and ideas and hatching artistic plans. Dylan Thomas (1914–53) was a regular and established his hard-drinking reputation at this pub. It was Thomas who once said: 'An alcoholic is somebody you don't like who drinks as much as you do.' He often drank at the French House with the flamboyant painter Francis Bacon (1909–92) and Jeffrey Bernard (see THE COACH AND HORSES) was also a regular. To this day, the French House remains a favourite haunt of London bohemians.

Originally called the **York Minster,** the bar became the unofficial London headquarters of the Free French Forces after the first Frenchman to be granted a landlord's licence in London took over the Dean Street bar. It was this, of course, that led to the pub changing its name. During the Second World War, General Charles de Gaulle, along with other senior officers, was exiled in London after the German invasion of France. Their official headquarters was established at 4 Carlton Gardens, but de Gaulle and his generals would often use the **York Minster** in Dean Street as a place to eat and drink and from which to direct the troops of the French Resistance battling the Germans in Europe.

The Garibaldi

THE ITALIAN HERO WHO BECAME THE TOAST (AND BISCUIT) OF VICTORIAN ENGLAND

At the beginning of the nineteenth century, Italy was a collection of warring states. The person responsible for drawing them into one country was Giuseppe Garibaldi (1807–82), a soldier and politician who is credited with being the first international revolutionary, a nineteenth-century Che Guevara.

Born on 4 July 1807, Garibaldi joined the Carbonari (the 'Charcoal Burners'), a secret revolutionary organization dedicated to Italian nationalism, but in 1834 fled to Brazil when his part in a failed revolution led to his being condemned to death in his absence by a Genoese court. In 1841 Garibaldi travelled to Montevideo, Uruguay, where the Uruguayan Civil War had been raging for two years. There he raised an Italian legion and then spent the next six years defending the city against the forces of Uruguayan president Manuel Oribe. He also earned himself a reputation as a brave, if not reckless, soldier by leading uphill bayonet charges against forces that far outnumbered his.

Garibaldi's heart never strayed from his home country, however, and the revolutions of 1848 finally tempted him home to Italy and to Milan in particular, where the inhabitants were fighting against Austrian occupation. When the French, under the command of the future Napoleon III, sent forces to Rome, Garibaldi's republican army found itself fighting the imperialists on far too many fronts. He was forced to withdraw his 4,000 men and head north to Venice, which was being besieged by the Austrians.

During this time his romantic profile as a freedom fighter was increasing daily, especially in Britain where Italian exiles frequently wrote about his exploits. Garibaldi himself was aware of the importance of public support and at one point had a press corps of nearly one hundred reporters travelling with his army. But with the Austrians, French and Spanish in hot pursuit, the people who wanted to write about him began to outnumber the people who wanted to fight alongside him and he was again forced into exile, this time to New York, on 30 July 1850.

Refusing a parade, the famous Italian managed to slip quietly into the city, where he retained a low profile, avoiding publicity for nearly three years before leaving Baltimore and sailing into Tyneside on 24 March 1854. Garibaldi cut quite a dash with his red silk shirt, poncho and sombrero hat. By mixing with the working classes rather than hobnobbing with local dignitaries, he further enhanced his reputation in the eyes of the public.

Garibaldi toured the country for a month, and thousands of Londoners were at Nine Elms station to greet his train when he arrived in the capital. He was hailed in the newspapers as the 'Italian lion' and 'the noblest Roman of them all'. Cake makers Peek Frean later developed a biscuit in his honour, said to be based on the raisin bread he provided for his marching troops and still produce the famous Garibaldi, or 'squashed fly', biscuits today. Thousands lined the streets, chanting 'We'll get a rope and hang the Pope, so up with Garibaldi' as the Italian hero passed by. Hotels made a profit from selling his bathwater and hundreds of Italian café and tavern owners renamed their establishments in his honour, such was his reputation during the 1850s. However, the great and the good of British establishment were relieved when the man they considered to be nothing more than a rabble-rousing terrorist returned, once again, to his homeland, with Queen Victoria declaring, 'Garibaldi, thank God, has gone.'

Back in the Mediterranean, Garibaldi bought the small island of Caprera, northern Sardinia, and in 1859, as the Second War of Independence broke out, he formed his own volunteer unit, the Hunters of the Alps. The Garibaldini, as the men were nicknamed, soon became a formidable force.

With his army growing on a daily basis both in number and support, he began moving north until, on 30 September 1860, the Garibaldini fought the French at Volturno and won a decisive victory. Garibaldi then handed over his southern territorial gains to Vittorio Emanuele, whom he famously addressed on 26 October as the 'King of Italy'.

With Garibaldi's dream of a free and united Italy finally a reality, the famous guerrilla leader rode triumphantly alongside the king into Naples on 7 November before retiring to Caprera in search of a more peaceful existence. But the political turmoil in Europe during the mid nineteenth century never really settled down and Garibaldi was called into action many more times. Despite this, he died peacefully in bed on 2 June 1882, aged seventy-four. Giuseppe Garibaldi is now regarded as the father of Italy, while to Victorian Britain he seemed like a latter-day Robin Hood.

The enthusiasim for him and for Victoria's other bête noire Lord Palmerston show a much less respectable side to nineteenth-century hero worship. Perhaps that's why there remain so many pubs called after him today.

The George

SLOW AND STEADY WINS THE ENGLISH THRONE

Britain is full of pubs called the George, the person on each sign differing from pub to pub. I've seen every well-known George on them, from George Best to Boy George. But who was the original George who inspired all these imitations?

The answer is quite simple: he was in fact King George I, and the sheer quantity of pubs named after him reflects the enormous public relief at the ending of a particularly turbulent period of English history. The turbulence was caused largely by the various foibles of the ruling Stuart dynasty. When Charles II died, in 1685, he left several illegitimate children behind him but no legal heir and so his brother James became king. He was not a popular choice. Charles's deathbed conversion to Catholicism and James's barely concealed adherence to the faith panicked a Protestant people who had been brought up on the highly coloured stories of inquisition and torture of Foxe's *Book of Martyrs*. Like his brother, James also had no male heir, or not at first, but by the time his wife had given birth to the long-awaited son, it was too late and rumours abounded that the baby was not his but part of a Catholic strategy to take over England.

In 1688 a group of nobles invited the Protestant William

of Orange, who was married to James's daughter Mary, to come to England with an army. When William arrived in November, many of James's key advisers and his other daughter, Anne, promptly defected to his side. James went into exile and William and Mary took over the throne. They didn't have any children and when they died, Anne succeeded them. Anne was pregnant a staggering eighteen times but tragically none of her babies lived longer than six months and when she died the crown passed to her obscure German cousin, George, the Elector of Hanover. Although fifty-seven Catholics bore a closer blood relationship to Anne, the Act of Settlement passed by an anxious Parliament in 1701 prohibited Catholics from inheriting the throne, and George was Anne's closest living Protestant relative.

Despite sharing a name with England's patron saint, George was a rather desperate choice for a xenophobic country racked by dissension and rebellion – and the Jacobites promptly tried to depose him for James's son (see THE THREE LORDS) – but he actually turned out to be a reasonable king. Although he didn't speak English, he had a lot of experience in governing. Parliament had chosen him and so, unlike his predecessors, he interfered relatively little with it. His citizens were ambivalent about their stolid king but knew that he was the best choice. As the author William Makepeace Thackeray put it a century later:

His heart was in Hanover. He was more than fifty-four years of age when he came amongst us: we took him because we wanted him, because he served our turn; we laughed at his uncouth German ways, and sneered at him ... I, for one, would have been on his side in those days.

Cynical, and selfish, as he was, he was better than [James's son the Old Pretender] with a French King's orders in his pocket, and a swarm of Jesuits in his train.

George's reign marked the end of absolute monarchy, and the combination of king and Parliament for the most part working together meant that England became more stable and more successful than ever before. It's ironic that it took a German king to stress the importance of British nationalism (see also THE BRITANNIA), but George's broader outlook led him to realize the potential that existed in a truly united kingdom. He was succeeded by Georges II, III and IV, and the stability never wavered. The name George thus became synonymous with the British crown at its steadiest; calling your inn the George was therefore an explicit expression of support for the status quo.

The George and Dragon

GOD FOR HARRY, ENGLAND AND SAINT GEORGE!

St George was not England's first patron saint (see THE CROWN AND ARROWS); he was adopted by Edward III around 1340 when the king dedicated the chapel he was building at Windsor to the soldier saint who represented the knightly virtues of chivalry he so admired.

Much of the rise in popularity of the legend of St George arose during the Crusades, the medieval religious wars waged by the Christians against their Muslim enemy in the East, from which the legend is believed to originate. The new taste was for much less passive saints and a more bloodthirsty Christianity, promoted by the clerics who accompanied the soldiers on the Crusades and who recruited huge numbers to the cause. So it must have been some comfort to know, before setting off into the unknown, that there were mighty Christian warriors, one called George, already there, and fighting for your own god.

The George and Dragon legend continued to grow in popularity in the Middle Ages thanks to a twelfth-century collection of saints' lives called *The Golden Legend*, written by Jacobus de Voragine in around 1260. The tale it recounts is set near a godless, pagan city called Silene, thought to be in what is now Libya. In a lake close to this city lived a fearsome dragon which threatened to kill the villagers if they did not provide it with a live animal to eat each day. And so, to appease the monster, they threw it a sheep every evening. When they had run out of sheep they drew lots as to which children to sacrifice instead. Eventually the king's own daughter was chosen: he pleaded with his people and promised them all of his gold and half of his land if they would spare her from the dragon, but they refused.

Standing at the edge of the lake, the trembling princess

saw a magnificent young Christian warrior from a nearby town riding towards her, having heard of the king's plight. 'I will defend you in the name of Jesus Christ,' he called as he galloped towards the dragon, which was, by then, approaching his supper. The dragon turned on George instead but, making the sign of the cross to protect himself, the warrior drove his lance into the neck of the beast with such force the creature was pinned to the ground.

George and the girl then walked the defeated dragon through the town to show the shamed creature to the people. He told them the Lord had sent him to deliver them all from evil and promised to slay the beast if they would become Christians like himself. The people agreed and the dragon was killed with one mighty blow from the warrior's sword. On that very spot, 15,000 people were then baptized and the king later built a church to the Blessed Virgin Mary on the same site.

Looking at the story more closely, you can see how Christianity had simply appropriated the ancient Greek tale of Perseus and Andromeda. The legend of St George held firm in England, but likewise, thanks to medieval myth and fable, the story developed and altered over the ages to suit changing tastes and needs. St George could be co-opted for all sorts of purposes, including folk remedies – as exemplified by a fifteenth-century manuscript advising people how to protect their horses from witches. At the time it was commonly believed that if a horse was found to be sweating, or tired, in the morning, then a witch or hag had stolen it during the night and ridden the animal hard. To prevent this, according to the manuscript, you should hang a flint with a small hole in the middle above the stable door to remind the witch, if she appeared in the night, that St George had banished her for all time. And apparently that worked.

The story of St George remained extremely popular, leading to later embellishment by Richard Johnson in his *Famous History of the Seven Champions of Christendom* (1596). Johnson removed most of the Christian religious references and replaced them with chivalrous and noble ideals, reflecting the romantic era of the knights and the Crusades. According to this version, George is a lad born in Coventry to aristocratic parents but is stolen soon after birth and taken east. As he grows up he bravely saves the King of Egypt's daughter, Princess Sabra, from a fearsome dragon and as a reward is told of his true ancestry. With that he returns to Coventry (rather than being sent there) where, before long, he is unlucky enough to encounter another dragon on Dunsmore Heath in Warwickshire. Although George manages to save the people by slaying this second dragon, he is himself poisoned by the beast's evil breath during the battle and dies soon afterwards, in the process securing a place in English folklore for ever more. His body, Johnson writes, is buried in the Chapel at Windsor that Edward III had dedicated to him.

And so the legend of the exploits of St George – possibly a form of early propaganda intended to bolster Crusader morale, later adopted by Edward III as he revised his military machine, making George the patron saint of England in the process – became part of English folklore, accounting for why you may have a pub or hotel near you bearing that name. (Interestingly, the St George's cross that forms the flag of England was originally the flag of Genoa, adopted by the City of London in 1190 so that English ships would be protected by the

Genoese fleet when they entered the Mediterranean. It was then taken up by the English soldiers during the later Crusades as the insignia for their uniform – hence its association with St George as a crusading knight.)

Despite coming from Libya and being the patron saint of several other exotic places ranging from Beirut to Brazil to Bulgaria, St George remains the epitome of English patriotism. The king's rallying cry at the Battle of AGINCOURT in Shakespeare's *Henry V* – 'God for Harry, England and Saint George!' (Act 3, Scene 1) – offers up a memorable trilogy for victory, especially during time of actual war. St George's Day in England falls every year on 23 April, which is incidentally also the day of Shakespeare was both born on and on which he died.

The Goat and Compass

A BIBLICAL SCAPEGOAT OR A MASONIC SYMBOL?

The Goat and Compass

The origin of this popular pub name (also rendered the **Goat and Compasses**) could have a number of different sources, foremost being the idea that it is a corruption of the phrase 'God encompasses us'. But written evidence for this can be found only in one place – a book by Anthony Trollope, who refers to the pub name in his novel *Framley Parsonage* (1861):

> . . . he came to a public-house. It was called the Goat and Compasses – a very meaningless name, one would say; but the house boasted of being a place of public entertainment very long established upon that site, having been a tavern in the days of Cromwell. At that time the pious landlord, putting up a pious legend for the benefit
>
> of his pious customers, had declared that – 'God encompasseth us.'

Trollope is clearly suggesting how the pub's name could have become corrupted over time. The theory is a neat and appealing one, but unfortunately there is no further proof to back it up.

Charles Swift explains in his book *Inns and Inn Signs*, written in 1936, that the name could have come from the belief in medieval times that goats could take on the illness and hard luck that would otherwise affect others. Country folk would traditionally keep a goat with other cattle, believing any illness among the herd would be absorbed by the poor goat, leaving the herd free of disease. Some even kept a goat inside the house of a sick person for this purpose. The following address might also be delivered at such a time: 'The goat that compass thee around is needful for compassing this end. That through whose compassment ye may be changed, from pain to happiness, disease to health.'

The belief that goats can shoulder the responsibility of the ills and misfortune of others has its origins in the Hebrew ritual for the Day of Atonement, in which two goats were presented to the altar of the tabernacle where the high priest would draw lots for the Lord and for Azazel, the desert demon (usually depicted with goat's horns, rather like the Devil). The goat selected to represent the Lord would then be sacrificed and, by taking confession, the high priest could transfer the people's sins to the second goat, which would then be banished to the wilderness, taking all the sins with it. In other words, the lucky goat had escaped sacrifice and became known as the escaped goat, or scapegoat, the expression we still use when blaming someone else for our mistakes or passing on what we should accept as our own responsibility.

A more likely reason the Goat and Compasses is used as a sign to represent an alehouse is connected with the historic livery companies of London – two in particular (but see also THE ELEPHANT AND CASTLE and THE SWAN WITH TWO NECKS). The Worshipful Company of Cordwainers (established in 1272) – leather workers using fine goatskin imported from Cordoba in Spain – has a crest with three goats' heads proudly displayed, while the Worshipful Company of Carpenters (founded in 1271) has three compasses on their crest. Could it be that these two groups of tradesmen, one established only a year after the other, had their own tavern distinguished by a sign bearing their joined crests?

Another suggestion is that the name may originate

with the Freemasons, whose symbol consists of a set square and compasses (to denote the tools of the stonemason) and who allegedly used a goat in their initiation ceremonies. Could it be, then, that, rather like other pubs associated with an ancient order (see THE FORESTERS' ARMS and THE ODDFELLOWS' ARMS), a tavern bearing the sign of the goat and compasses was advertising itself as a venue for Freemasons? Whoever its sign was originally aimed at – cordwainers, carpenters or Freemasons – the Goat and Compasses represents a place of escape, although sadly not for goats.

The Golden Hind
FAMOUS SHIP OF THE ORIGINAL 'PIRATE' OF THE CARIBBEAN

The many pubs bearing the name the Golden Hind do so in commemoration of the celebrated ship (historically spelled *Golden Hinde*) belonging to Britain's most famous sailor. Born near Tavistock in Devon sometime around 1540, Francis Drake was the son of a farmer and Protestant preacher. By the time he was nine, the family had been caught up in the Prayer Book Rebellion, and had to flee Devon for the safety of Kent. Aged thirteen, he was apprenticed to a ship trading between London and European ports. Drake proved such a talented sailor that, by the age of twenty, he was already the owner and captain of his own vessel. Like his father, he was a committed Protestant and implacable foe of the Catholic Spanish; this suited his occupation, which was to raid Spanish ports and ships and seize their possessions. After Drake was ambushed in the Mexican port San Juan de Ulua, in the Caribbean, he and his cousin John Hawkins swore vengeance on the Spanish that they attempted to wreak for the rest of their lives. In 1573 Drake tracked down and intercepted the 'silver train', a convoy of mules and donkeys carrying a vast fortune in precious metals and spices. The Spanish called him El Draque (the Dragon), based on their pronunciation of 'Drake': Philip II is reputed to have offered a reward of 20,000 ducats (equivalent to about £4 million today) for his life. Returning to England with a cargo of Spanish treasure, Drake received a hero's welcome.

In 1577 Queen Elizabeth I, by then realizing the riches the wider world had to offer, raised funds for an expedition to South America and beyond. A brave move as the costs involved were astronomical and there was every chance nothing of interest, or value, would be discovered. Imagine the Queen today personally paying for an expedition into space to find out what lies beyond the reaches of the Hubble Telescope.

Francis Drake's reputation as a sailor and adventurer had risen over the previous years and his hatred of the Spanish was also well known. With Elizabeth's personal support Drake was no longer a simple pirate; he now had a mandate to attack the Spanish in the name of the crown wherever he encountered their ships, including along the Spanish-owned coast of South America, helping himself to whatever he could lay his hands on. It was still piracy, of course, albeit state-sponsored, with the full authority of the English queen and the protection of her navy, and that was obviously something that appealed to Drake immensely.

Drake reached the Brazilian coast by the spring of 1578. After taking on water and food supplies, he performed a small ceremony, renaming his flag ship *Pelican* the *Golden Hind* in honour of the voyage's principal financial backer, Sir Christopher Hatton, a wealthy English politician, Lord Chancellor (1587–91) and, some believe, a lover of the queen herself. The hind, or female deer, featured prominently on Hatton's coat of arms. Having navigated the Straits of Magellan, the first Englishman to do so, Drake and his *Golden Hind* plundered the Spanish ports on the Pacific coast of South America and sailed as far north as (what would later be named) San Francisco Bay, which he claimed for the queen in the name of 'New Albion' (see THE ALBION for more on the origins of this name).

Drake continued west, more out of curiosity than anything else as no man had done so before, and by the end of 1579 he had sailed past the Philippines, Indonesia and navigated the Indian Ocean back to the more familiar seas around the Cape of Good Hope. The *Golden Hind* then headed home, arriving in Plymouth in September 1580, laden with spices and other treasures, with Drake having become the first Englishman to circumnavigate the globe. A few months later Queen Elizabeth boarded the *Golden Hind* and knighted the most famous sailor of them all. Which isn't too surprising as the queen's own share of Drake's booty amounted to around £160,000, enough to pay off her entire foreign debt and have £40,000 left over, an unimaginable sum in 1580. Elizabeth ordered all written accounts of Drake's voyage to be considered classified information, and its participants sworn to silence on pain of death; her aim was to keep Drake's activities away from the eyes of arch-rival Spain.

The Spanish, however, were not impressed with the English buccaneer and wanted revenge and their money back. In 1587, with the Spanish preparing for war with England, Drake once again took matters into his own hands and surprised the Spanish with a pre-emptive strike at Cadiz by sending fire ships into the harbour, effectively destroying the Spanish fleet in a single night.

The Singeing of the King of Spain's Beard (as the raid became known) left the Spanish furious and within a year they had assembled the famous Armada to take revenge on the English fleet, in particular Sir Francis Drake, off the coast of Plymouth. The famous story of Drake's reluctance to interrupt a game of bowls when the Spanish ships were sighted is an iconic example of British sangfroid in the face of danger, although it is likely to have been invented for use as propaganda. The English fleet was hopelessly outnumbered, but, helped by a luckily timed storm, Drake, under the command of Lord Howard, managed to crush the Spanish. In the end fewer than half of the Armada's 130 ships returned safely to Cadiz.

Drake continued seafaring all his life, although his later campaigns lacked the success of his earlier ones. He died in 1596 while anchored off the coast of Portobelo, Panama, and was buried at sea in a lead coffin. There is a legend that if England is ever in danger, beating on Drake's drum will cause him to come back and save the country.

The Green Man

THE PAGAN FERTILITY SYMBOL ADORNING CHURCHES AND PUBS ALIKE

A popular name for a country pub, the Green Man is possibly the oldest figure in English folklore. His image can

be found in the architecture of medieval cathedrals and churches all over Europe. In this form, it's only his head that's depicted, usually wreathed in greenery – branches, leaves or vines, in some cases sprouting from his eyes, ears and nose. The foliage is frequently recognizable as oak or hawthorn (called the 'May tree' because it blossoms in that month) and the face is generally severe, with a decided frown. The Green Man is commonly believed to be an ancient fertility symbol, predating organized religion, but then the Church, pragmatically, has never been slow to embrace images and ideas from other cultures and claim them as its own.

In fact, as Christianity grew throughout Europe, missionaries often deliberately assimilated pagan stories and beliefs in an effort to encourage conversion. Christ's birthday is now commonly thought to have been in September, for instance, but the dates of Christmas usefully coincide with Yule and other midwinter festivals. In some cases, churches were built on ancient pagan sites, often on the very foundations. All of which indicates a far stronger pagan element in modern Christianity than many Christians would care to admit.

Because of his association with rebirth, representing the new growth of spring, some Christians adopted the Green Man as a symbol of Easter (itself a pagan festival, relating to the goddess Eostre, celebrated at the spring equinox) and of the resurrection, although it comes as no real surprise that others regard him as a demon or even the devil. Many equate the Green Man with Jack-in-the-Green, the May King of traditional British May Day cere-monies, who wreathed himself with green leaves and flowers, feigned death and then came to life, jumping up to console his disconsolate May Queen and dance with her. There is also evidence to suggest the Green Man existed in the traditions of many ancient cultures and belongs to no single country. Outside Europe similar figures have been found in the Middle East and further afield, in Nepal, India and Borneo.

Before Christianity, the ancient Britons worshipped trees, believing protective spirits to live inside them. People in need of good fortune would make a pilgrimage to a designated tree and stroke or hug it, leading to the traditional expression 'touch wood' when we are hoping for a little luck to come our way. The Celts considered the Green Man to be the god of spring and summer, disappearing each autumn for the long harsh winter, before returning again in the spring to provide warmth and crops, and the pagan festival of Beltane held on 1 May every year celebrates this. May Day was a holiday throughout Europe – and a great excuse for a day of drunkenness and celebration, thus making the Green Man an ideal name for a pub.

The Green Man is also associated with one of the greatest English folk heroes of them all – ROBIN HOOD, whose image also appears on many a pub sign. Both live in the woods and dress all in green; indeed, it's thought Robin Hood and his adventures may have arisen from the myth of the Green Man. The Green Man has also been linked with Robin Goodfellow, more familiar as Puck, the mischievous nature spirit immortalized in Shakespeare's *A Midsummer Night's Dream*.

The Green Man could be connected, too, with the Green Knight, of Arthurian legend, whose story is told in the fourteenth-century poem *Sir Gawain and the Green Knight*. In this tale, a man clad completely in green, and even with a green beard, hair and skin, strides into the court of King Arthur on New Year's Day and issues a challenge. He asks for someone in the court to strike him once with his axe, on condition that he will return the blow one year and one day later. Sir Gawain accepts the challenge and severs the man's head at one stroke, expecting him to die. The Green Knight, however, picks up his head, reminds Gawain to meet him at the Green Chapel in a year and a day and rides away. When Gawain eventually, after many adventures, finds the knight and submits to his blow, he also escapes with his life, receiving only a small nick (which he could have avoided, it turns out, by not flirting with the Green Knight's wife a little earlier). The Green Knight then explains how the whole thing had been been set up by Arthur's evil sister, Morgan le Fay, always looking for an opportunity to make trouble, and they part on good terms.

Green Man – whether you regard him as a fertility symbol,
a nature god, Robin Hood, Puck or a figure from the time
of King Arthur – comes steeped in legend and folklore.

The Hansom Cab
(Kensington, London)

HORSE-DRAWN PREDECESSOR OF THE MODERN TAXI

The Hansom Cab pub, which served its first drink in
1810, claims to have been named in honour of Joseph
Aloysius Hansom (1803–83), designer and builder of the
popular hansom cabs used originally in London from
1834. Seeing as he was just seven at the time, it's more
likely the pub was renamed at a later date in honour of
the man who built the replacement to the more cumber-
some hackney carriage and exported his vehicle all over
Europe and the British Empire. By the way, the word
'cab' is in fact an abbreviation of 'cabriolet', an open-
topped horse-drawn carriage with a folding hood that
could cover two occupants during bad weather, the forerunner to the modern-day convertible sports car with a
soft top, also known as a cabriolet.

The hansom cab remained in use until the 1920s when
motorized transport and the London Underground began
to limit its effectiveness, and the last hansom cab was
licensed in 1947, after which the vehicles soon vanished
from our streets. Hansom was also responsible for building Birmingham Town Hall between 1833 and 1835,
although, having tendered a price that was too low for

the project, he was bankrupted in 1834. Luckily for him, he had already started work on his new cab design that would lead to wealth, fame and, most importantly, a pub named after his new invention.

Harry's Bar
THE WORLD-FAMOUS VENETIAN BAR BELOVED BY THE LITERATI (AND GLITERATI)

Although many traditional pub names came about hundreds of years ago and need a bit of explaining, the world's most famous bar is called, quite simply, Harry's Bar, which sounds straightforward enough but there's a quite a story behind it even so. The name has caught on, too: every Harry's Bar you walk into throughout the world derives its name from the original Harry's Bar, on Calle Vallaresso near St Mark's Square in Venice.

First opened in March 1931 by Giuseppe Cipriani, Harry's Bar became an instant success when Giuseppe's imaginative cocktails proved popular with young Venetians. However, with the outbreak of the Second World War, the fascist authorities prohibited the use of English names and Giuseppe was forced to change 'Harry' to 'Arrigo' (the Italian version of the name). Then, in 1943, the bar was closed to the public and became a mess hall for German and Italian officers. At the end of the war, as Europe slowly returned to normal and people began rebuilding their shattered lives, Cipriani reverted to the original name for his watering hole. Harry's Bar once again opened its doors to tourists and locals alike, immediately becoming popular with the likes of Noël Coward, Humphrey Bogart, Charlie Chaplin and the legendary film director Orson Welles, who placed the same order every time he visited, two bottles of champagne – and that was just for him.

But it is largely thanks to the writers among the clientele that Harry's Bar began to establish an international reputation, helped in particular by Ernest Hemingway, who had his own table in one corner and who immortalized the bar in his novel *Across the River and into the Trees* (1950), not to mention the short story 'In Harry's Bar in Venice'. It was Hemingway who came up with the name for one of Cipriani's now famous cocktails, the Montgomery, after the barman explained to the writer the recipe was fifteen parts gin and one part vermouth. Hemmingway noted that the proportion of gin to vermouth sounded like the odds General Montgomery once faced during the recent war, still managing to win despite being massively outnumbered.

Since the Second World War, the reputation of Harry's Bar has continued to spread and it serves a growing clientele, from celebrities and princes to lowly serfs like you and me. In 2001, in recognition of its status, the Italian Ministry for Cultural Affairs declared *the* Harry's Bar in Venice a national landmark.

Which brings me to the obvious question: who was Harry? During the roaring 1920s a rich American family decided to pack off one of their number to Europe in a bid to curb his enthusiasm for drinking. In 1929, in the care of his aunt and her Pekingese pooch, Harry Pickering moved into the Hotel Europa in Venice to begin his period of rehabilitation but, since his aunt liked a drink or two herself, the three of them idled most of their days at the hotel bar, at that time being run by twenty-nine-year-old

Giuseppe Cipriani, who later noted that any small bar could have made a decent profit just out of Harry and his aunt alone. Quite what possessed the family to send a young man to Italy to curb his drinking habits is anybody's guess, but within a few months the pair argued, the aunt flounced out, and Harry found himself alone in the city without the funds to pay even his drinks bill. Instead, the young man sat alone in the bar, gazing out of the window, until one day Giuseppe asked him what his problem was. On learning of the lad's plight, the barman chose to ignore the motto written behind the bar in so many pubs: 'Please don't ask for credit because a punch in the mouth often offends' and handed over his life savings of 10,000 lire so that Harry could have one last drink with him, pay his bills and book a boat home to Boston.

Giuseppe was soon reading in the newspapers about the stock market crash in America of October 1929 and the subsequent Great Depression that crippled the US economy. As the months passed the barman began to give up hope of ever seeing his money again, until one day, in February 1931, Harry strolled back into the Hotel Europa and placed 10,000 lire in cash on the bar, with the words: 'Here you are – thanks for the money.' The young man then pulled another 30,000 lire out of his pocket and handed it over to the astonished barman, saying: 'And now you can open a bar of your own.' Giuseppe Cipriani and Harry Pickering opened the doors to Harry's Bar on 13 May 1931, and if as many customers who claim to have walked through the door on that day had actually done so, then, as Cipriani himself later declared, 'I would have had to have a bar the size of St Mark's Square.'

The Hero of Inkerman
THE ORDINARY SOLDIER WHO KEPT HIS HEAD UNDER FIRE

Inkerman was one of the more famous battles in the Crimean War (see also THE ALMA). On 5 November 1854 Russian forces attacked the British at Inkerman, a key town commanding a major supply route, with around 30,000 men. The British and French forces of about 15,000 were hopelessly outnumbered but fought bravely and tenaciously, driving the Russians back and inflicting over 12,000 casualties on the Cossack army, some of whom retreated to the surrounding hills and caves and set up sniper positions, picking off the British in the town at will.

A division of men under the command of Corporal John Prettyjohn was sent to clear the caves of Cossack snipers and in so doing managed to run out of ammunition. Their situation was desperate. The *London Gazette* later published part of a letter written by Colonel Wesley, the Deputy Adjutant General:

·On 5th November 1854 at the Battle of Inkerman, Corporal Prettyjohn's platoon went to clear out some caves occupied by snipers. In doing so they used up almost all of their ammunition, and then noticed fresh parties of Russians creeping up the hill in single file. Corporal Prettyjohn gave instructions to his men to collect as many stones as possible which they could use instead of ammunition. When the first Russian appeared he was seized by the corporal and thrown down the slope. The rest were greeted by a hail of stones and retreated.

News of Prettyjohn's exploits were widely reported throughout Britain and the Hero of Inkerman was awarded the Victoria Cross for gallantry in the face of the enemy, the first Royal Marine ever to be so highly honoured. He also won the British Crimea Medal for action at Inkerman, Sebastopol and Balaclava, the Turkish and Sardinian Crimean Medals, the China Medal and a Good Conduct Gratuity for bravery in the Crimea. One reason for the popularity of the Hero of Inkerman as a pub name was that, unlike most British heroes, Prettyjohn wasn't of noble blood; he was just an ordinary man who had shown enormous courage and common sense in the face of danger.

Prettyjohn finally left the Royal Marines on 16 June 1865 after twenty-one years as a professional soldier and he moved with his family to Greater Manchester where he became golf club steward at the Whalley Range Bowls Club in Withington, Lancashire. Now I bet that is one golf club that never had to put up with slow players or ill-mannered guests.

The Hope and Anchor
AN UNLIKELY AID FOR KEEPING YOU BUOYANT?

As well as its obvious nautical associations (see THE ANCHOR), an anchor was an early Christian symbol of hope and security, as derived from the words of St Paul in Hebrews 6: 19: 'which hope we have as the anchor of the soul'. It was also the emblem of St Nicholas of Bari, the patron saint of sailors, and is associated with St Clement, Pope Clement I, martyred during the first century AD when he was tied to an anchor by the Romans and thrown

The Hope and Anchor

into the sea. Any of these religious references might have inspired an innkeeper to use a ship's anchor as a sign outside his establishment. It would also account for the variation the **Blue Anchor**, blue representing hope.

The Horse and Hounds

FROM A HUNT-LOVING MONARCH TO AN ARISTOCRATIC SABOTEUR

Once regarded as the typical English country pastime, fox hunting, like cricket, was transported across the world during the heyday of the British Empire. The hunt, with all its pomp and ritual, lives on in America, Canada, Russia, New Zealand and many European countries. In Britain the hunt continues, especially the Boxing Day 'meet', the hounds now following an artificial trail that

doesn't lead to a fox (or not intentionally). It is only the hunting of foxes with hounds that is affected by the ban. There's nothing to stop hunters shooting foxes or running them over with a horse.

Although the use of hounds to track and trap prey can be traced back to the ancient Egyptians, the earliest recorded fox hunt with hounds dates to 1534 when farmers in Norfolk sent their dogs out to hunt and kill foxes in an attempt to control the 'vermin'. There is no doubt a single hungry fox can decimate a hen house in minutes if the crafty pest can get into one, and country folk, quite understandably, should be able to do what they can to protect their livestock. It is difficult to find anybody who seriously disagrees with this sentiment. The main objection, albeit shrouded in a veil of animal rights concern, appears to be to the vulgar spectacle of the landed gentry in their red tunics, blowing their bugles and galloping over the countryside with packs of hounds ripping foxes apart, all in the name of 'pest control'. The city law-makers, argue country folk, don't understand the countryside and the problems caused by pests. Meanwhile, city folk argue that country people don't understand the cities and the problems caused by pests living there, either.

It was Charles II who encouraged the training of hounds to hunt foxes, and the king himself was an enthusiastic fan of the hunt – perhaps in retaliation for all those years he spent at bay. It is recorded that one of his closest friends, George Villiers, 2nd DUKE OF BUCKINGHAM (1628–87), established the first organized hunt during his time at court. Their side's losing of the English Civil War following the Battle of Worcester in 1651 ensured that both men experienced what it was like to be hunted (see THE ROYAL OAK); like the king, George managed to go to ground, however, escaping to Europe in the aftermath of the war. Following the restoration of the monarchy in 1660, when both men had emerged from exile, they were keen to be on the side of the hunters once again. Thanks to the new king's fondness for the sport, fox hunting with horses and hounds became a national pastime, along with the familiar appearance of horses and hounds milling around taverns and inns that still bear the name to this day.

But there was also opposition to fox hunting, long before the twenty-first century. The original hunt saboteurs found that hunts could be thrown into disarray via a rather strange means – using a smelly fish. Herring has long been one of the most widely caught fish in the seas around Britain. In the days before refrigeration, herring and mackerel were preserved by a process of heavy salting and smoking to ensure the fish were still edible by the time they arrived in the inland market towns. This process, also known as kippering, turns the herring a deep reddish brown and heightens its already strong smell. Dragging these pungent fish over the fields was found to confuse the hounds, which would follow the scent of the herring rather than that of the fox, and it led to the expression 'red herring', meaning a false trail, becoming established in the English language.

Back in the nineteenth century, an English lord who resented hunters riding their horses all over his fields in pursuit of foxes paid one of his farm workers an extra shilling to lay a trail of herring that would lead the hounds away from his land. On the morning of the hunt, the lad did exactly what was asked of him and laid a fishy trail down across the fields, through the wooded glade, over the hedge, through the meadow and past the river. After several hours he decided to take a break and popped into the local pub, called ironically enough the **Fox and Hounds**, for a bite to eat and a pint or two. Before long, the distant sound of barking dogs could be heard and the lad grinned as the noise grew louder: his plan had clearly worked. But they were getting a little close for comfort now and he became alarmed as they drew into view outside the pub. Looking down, he realized he still had his bag of herring with him, but it was too late: the hounds poured into the pub and tore him and several other customers to shreds.

The Iron Duke
FROM STEELY COMMANDER TO UNBENDING PRIME MINISTER

All over Britain there are pubs dedicated to one man. When an establishment is called the **Wellington** or the

Duke of Wellington, it is clear to see who it's named after and the regard in which one of our greatest military heroes is still held. Calling a pub the Iron Duke, on the other hand, shows a rather more ambivalent reaction to his legacy.

Arthur Wellesley (1769–1852) is most famous for having finally crushed Napoleon at Waterloo, Belgium, in 1815, thus concluding the little Frenchman's domination of Europe and changing the course of history in the process. The outcome could have been very different, however, and Wellington himself later admitted the battle was 'the nearest-run thing you ever saw in your life'. Wellesley was renowned for his courage in the line of fire, and had served the army with distinction in the Netherlands and India before returning to England and becoming MP for Newport on the Isle of Wight in 1807. His political rise was swift and within two years had been appointed a privy counsellor (one of a body of select and powerful advisers to the British sovereign), although his comfortable life in Westminster came to an abrupt halt when he was recalled to the army and charged with the task of confronting the Napoleonic threat to Britain and the rest of Europe. It was in the Peninsula War, fought in Portugal and Spain, that he achieved his greatest military success, winning a number of important victories and being granted a dukedom following Napoleon's exile to Elba in 1814.

Returning to England after the Battle of Waterloo, Wellington re-entered politics. His reputation as a military leader guaranteed his rise to power over the next few years and he became prime minister in 1828. Unfortunately, the very qualities that had made him such a successful general ensured his swift decline in popularity as a politician. At a time when reform was sorely needed, he was highly conservative, the spectre of the French Revolution making him suspicious of giving too much ground to the common people (this was before the working classes had the vote). Unrest had already shown itself following the end of the Napoleonic Wars, with famine and widespread unemployment, not helped by the imposition of the Corn Laws (in which cheaper foreign wheat was banned in order to force people to buy the more expensive British variety). Things had come to a head on 16 August 1819 when a crowd of nearly 80,000 protestors gathered for a meeting at St Peter's Field in Manchester. The military was called in and the ensuing sabre-drawn charge by the cavalry left fifteen citizens dead and 700 badly injured. The massacre became known as Peterloo in a mocking echo of the Battle of Waterloo, which may have brought peace but hadn't delivered prosperity or a more equal society.

As economic conditions deteriorated and unemployment increased over the following decade, the mood in the rural areas was often volatile, leading in 1830 to the Swing Riots, a widespread uprising among agricultural labourers who feared their livelihoods were under threat from the newly introduced threshing machines (see also THE TROUBLE HOUSE). During an emergency debate in the House of Lords it was suggested by Earl Grey, the leader of the Whig party, that parliamentary reform was the best way to end the violence. Prime Minister Wellington responded that the (obviously flawed) constitution was 'near perfect' and could not be improved upon and there was no need of parliamentary reform. When news of this reached the streets, rioters turned their attack on his London home, Apsley House (or, as it is better known these days, Number

One, London), and Wellington was forced to install heavy iron shutters to prevent his windows being shattered and his house looted. It was this and not his legendary steeliness or battlefield resolve that earned the, by then, deeply unpopular war hero the nickname the Iron Duke.

Jack Straw's Castle
(Hampstead, London)

WHY THE POLL TAX PROVED THE FINAL STRAW FOR ENGLAND'S PEASANTS

One of the best-known pub names in London, Jack Straw's Castle has nothing to do with the eponymous Labour MP, real name John Whitaker Straw, who allegedly changed it

JACK STRAW'S CASTLE

to Jack to associate himself with the romantic reputation of the first Jack Straw, one of England's first socialists. Today Wat Tyler is chiefly remembered as the leader of the Peasants' Revolt, but at the time Jack Straw was seen as the real hero.

The second half of the fourteenth century was a time of huge change. When the Black Death had killed off nearly a third of the population of Europe between 1348 and 1350, it had also freed the survivors from the feudal system, allowing them for the first time to work for whomever they chose and to charge as much as they liked. A panicked government passed a law that fixed wages and forbade peasants from leaving their villages. Those that ignored the law were heavily punished, but there was growing resentment among the workers at the unfairness of it all. The church was going through similar struggles, with popular figures like John Wycliffe campaigning for reform, insisting that the Church should give its monies back to the people rather than demanding further revenue in the form of huge taxes. The introduction of a new poll tax in 1379, ostensibly to finance a military campaign overseas, as part of the Hundred Years' War (see also THE AGINCOURT), was to prove the final straw.

On 30 May 1381 a government bailiff arrived in the village of Fobbing in Essex to collect the tax, which had recently risen from one groat per person to three. He was met by a group of villagers led by local landowner Thomas Baker, who ran him out of town. When Robert Belknap, the chief justice, was sent to investigate the incident and punish the offenders, he too was attacked and had to beat a retreat, empty-handed, back to London.

The protest now spreading, Jack Straw, a former

preacher, gathered the men of Essex at Great Baddow to march on London. In Kent, Wat Tyler, a blacksmith and former soldier, was doing the same. Things escalated when on 14 June a group of peasants stormed the Tower of London and executed Simon of Sudbury, the Lord Chancellor (seen as partially responsible for the poll tax) and Archbishop of Canterbury. Many believe they were actually let in by sympathetic guards, who did nothing to protect the unpopular archbishop.

By the time Wat Tyler and Jack Straw met in London, they had gathered an army of over 60,000 people, a serious threat to Richard II and, the king being only fourteen at the time, his regent John of Gaunt (see THE RED LION). King Richard bravely rode out with a small entourage to meet with the revolting peasants at Smithfield, the site of today's famous meat market in London. Things might have turned out very differently if Straw had then taken the lead rather than Wat Tyler. Tyler, who had fought under the Black Prince at Crécy (see THE STAR AND GARTER), believed strongly that if the king heard the peasants' woes he would change the laws and help them; Jack Straw, by contrast, had no such faith in royalty, and may have been more wary in his dealings with the king.

An overconfident (and rather starstruck) Tyler rode forward alone to meet the king. The royal entourage surrounded him and William Walworth, the Lord Mayor of London, drew his sword and ran the peasant through, killing him instantly. The young king then rode alone to the peasant army and assured the mob that their demands had been met and Tyler had been knighted, famously adding: 'You shall have no captain but me.' (Which was true, of course, now that Tyler was dead, but any ambiguity went unnoticed.)

Apparently satisfied, the mob then left, dispersing and making their way back to their villages. With control soon re-established in the capital, the nobility were quick to react: breaking every promise the king had made, they gathered a force of 7,000 armed men and pursued the ring-leaders back into the countryside with ruthless brutality.

The end of the Peasants' Revolt of 1381 was marked when Jack Straw was caught and beheaded, after apparently confessing (under torture) that the real intention of the marchers was to kill the king, bishops, all landowners and rectors of churches. He rapidly became a symbol of the common man rebelling against the oppression of the complacent state. He is even mentioned in *The Canterbury Tales* – written by Geoffrey Chaucer in the late fourteenth century, not long after the Revolt – as a leader of rebels protesting against foreign workers. As I write this, six hundred years later, I see British oil-refinery workers are striking in Lincolnshire over the use of foreign workers and wonder why nothing has been learned.

A popular play written in 1593 called *The Life and Death of Jack Straw* includes a scene where Straw incites his men to rebellion, crying: 'The king, God wot, knows not what's done by such poor men as we, / But we'll make him know it, if you will be ruled by me.' The setting is Hampstead Heath (perhaps on the very spot currently occupied by the modern pub), the rebel leader addressing the mob from on top of a loaded hay wagon, which became jokingly known as Jack Straw's Castle as it was as close as any peasant, Jack Straw included, was likely to get to owning a real castle.

Back in 1721, when the pub was founded, its choice of name was a daring one, even then, still popular with the independent-minded workforce of London but less so with the authorities. The lesser-known **Wat Tyler**, in Dartford, Kent, is also a reference to the same historic event of 1381.

125

The John Barleycorn

The John Barleycorn
FROM TRADITIONAL RHYME TO PUB ANTHEM

John Barleycorn is the hero of a traditional English folk-song dating as far back as we can trace. A version appeared in the *Bannatyne Manuscript* of 1586 (a collection of Scottish poems named after its sixteenth-century compiler, George Bannatyne) and many variations have been published since, including one penned by another Scot, the poet Robert Burns, in 1782, and upon which most subsequent versions of the song are based.

In the song, John Barleycorn's death is prophesied and then enacted in various grisly ways; he then comes back to life again. It has been interpreted as pagan practice or a more symbolic type of sacrifice as enacted in fertility rituals to ensure the return of summer after winter (see also THE GREEN MAN and THE RISING SUN). Indeed, due to his suffering and resurrection, many folklorists have compared John Barleycorn to Christ. A simpler interpretation is that he is the personification of the barley, which needs to be buried under the earth to grow again:

There were three men come out o' the west their fortunes for to try, And these three men made a solemn vow, John Barleycorn must die. They ploughed, they sowed, they harrowed him in, throwed clods upon his head, And these three men made a solemn vow, John Barleycorn was dead.

Barley is a crucial crop, both for eating and drinking. In malted form it provides the vital ingredient for both whisky and beer (see THE MALTINGS and THE WHEATSHEAF). The song thus is the pub hymn. In an echo of Jesus's body and blood being represented by the host (bread) and wine of the Holy Communion, John Barleycorn's body and blood become, quite literally, bread and beer.

The John Company
THE COMPANY THAT RULED A SUBCONTINENT

Pubs calling themselves the John Company do so in reference to the nickname for the East India Company (see also THE BOMBAY GRAB), which was set up in 1600 by Elizabeth I. Trading in cotton, silk, tea and opium, the East India Company became fabulously wealthy and powerful over the next three centuries. In the process it also became far more than just a company. When local Indian rulers started rebelling against the foreign exploitation of a wealth that had once been theirs, the company built up an army. And when the Nawab of Bengal and his French allies seized Fort William, Calcutta, in 1756, they decided to strike. The popularity of their cause was helped enormously by public outrage back in Britain at the 'Black Hole of Calcutta' incident in which the Nawab's soldiers had crammed 146 British prisoners into one tiny cell and only twenty-three survived the night. The facts are now disputed but at the time they were a public relations coup for the East India Company, meaning that they were free to act as they saw fit, without question and with public support.

After the inglorious Battle of Plassey in 1757, where Robert Clive's outnumbered forces mainly prevailed by bribing the general in charge of most of the Indian armies not to attack, the Company came to rule large tracts of India, exercising military power and taking administrative control.

A series of further wars were won by the company and their powers over the subcontinent lasted until 1858, when, following the events of the Indian Rebellion of 1857, the British crown assumed direct administration of India in the new British Raj, and thus the John Company became part of the John Bull Corporation.

The John Paul Jones

HOW AN AMERICAN INVASION WAS FOILED BY A LOCK-IN AT AN ENGLISH PUB

John Paul Jones (1747–92) always hated the English. Born in a devastated Scotland (the English had imposed very harsh punishments in retaliation for the recent Jacobite Risings – see THE THREE LORDS), he went to sea at the age of thirteen, sailing from the northern English port of Whitehaven in Cumbria. By the age of twenty-one, and after serving in a number of slave ships, Jones had become disillusioned with the cruel trade, so he jumped ship in Barbados and made his way back to Scotland. He soon found another ship and, having proved his skill as a navigator when he unexpectedly had to take over as captain, was put in charge of his own vessel. All went well at first but then he was accused of killing two of his sailors, after quarrels and problems with discipline, and everything started to go wrong.

With his reputation fast slipping from glowing to notorious, Jones decided in 1773 to leave his troubles behind and move to the New World. When the American War of Independence broke out only two years later (see also THE ADDISON ARMS and THE MOLLY PITCHER), Jones wasted no time in joining the American navy, despite the colonies having no ships of the line (custom-built warships). With few qualms about fighting his old masters, he was soon in action attacking British merchant ships along the north-eastern coast of America.

In November 1777 Jones was sent to Europe with orders to 'assist America wherever possible', and spent the next six months disrupting British shipping until finally, on 23 April 1778, the commander led his forces to attack the mainland at Whitehaven, the port he had first sailed from eighteen years earlier.

However, on arrival, his ship the *Ranger* had barely enough fuel left for their oil lamps let alone enough to start the fires they intended among the British fleet of over 300 anchored in the harbour. A small raiding party was set up with the task of stealing oil and other fuel from the local inn that no doubt Jones was familiar with from his youthful days in port. But, with discipline being what it was among eighteenth-century sailors, the men stopped for a few ales and ended up staying drinking with the locals until dawn. Eventually somebody gave their identity away and the Americans were forced back to the ship, where they raised anchor and ran. With the raid all but aborted, Jones instead sailed for St Mary's Isle, off the Scottish coast, where he intended to kidnap the Earl of Selkirk in the hope of exchanging his prisoner for captured American sailors. But the earl was not at home, so Jones's men ransacked his manor house instead.

News of these raids, albeit failures, damaged morale within the British forces and government as they showed that the Americans were prepared and able to attack the British mainland. As a result of this, Jones, a sailor from Scotland, was hailed as the first American naval hero and to this day is regarded as the father of the American navy. The raids are commemorated locally with pubs called the John Paul Jones both in Whitehaven and in Southerness, Scotland, close to the place of his birth.

The John Snow
(Soho, London)

WHY IT'S FAR SAFER TO STICK TO BEER

There is only one public house by this name, on Broad-wick Street in the heart of Soho, and it commemorates a local doctor, one John Snow (1813–58), who managed to save thousands of lives through his lateral thinking.

In the mid nineteenth century, London had a vast and growing population and yet no proper sanitation. Many basements had brimming cesspits underneath their floor-boards. The rich paid for water to be brought to their houses, the poorer gathered their own water from local pumps. This water was generally piped in from the extremely polluted River Thames, which at that time was little better than a vast open sewer. Waterborne disease, unsurprisingly enough, was rife – especially cholera and typhoid – but nobody knew how it was spread.

In August 1854, after several outbreaks of cholera had already sprung up throughout the capital, a major outbreak struck Soho. In its severest form, cholera is one of the most rapidly progressing diseases known to man: without prompt medical intervention, an infected person can die within three hours. During that outbreak in 1854, 127 people had died within three days. Over the course of the week, three-quarters of the inhabitants had fled, while those that remained were dropping like flies. Dr John Snow, tending the sick, was sceptical about the popular theories of the time, essentially that 'bad air', known as 'miasma', was responsible for spreading the disease. But he remained unable to explain exactly how the infection was passed so quickly between people who appeared to have no direct contact with each other.

Marking on a map the homes of as many of the victims as he could find, Snow made a startling discovery. Studying the map, he noticed that eighty-seven of the eighty-nine victims he had identified had all drunk water from a pump in Broad Street. By contrast, there had been no reports of the death from cholera of anyone who drank water from a different well, even if they lived close to Broad Street. Snow immediately took his findings to the local authorities, urging them to remove the pump handle. The authorities, believing like everyone else that 'bad air' was responsible for the disease, were initially reluctant as closing the pump would inconvenience local residents. But Snow managed to persuade them to remove the handle long enough at least for him to investigate further, as a result of which there were no new cases of cholera in the area. Snow then discovered that the well had been dug only three feet from an old cesspit that had begun to leak sewage directly into the water supply; this, he concluded, must be the source of the disease.

After the epidemic had halted, government officials still refused to acknowledge Snow's conclusions, terrified that if the public learned they had all been drinking infected water there would be riots. In 1848 John Snow published an essay, *On the Mode of Communication of Cholera*, in which he suggested the disease was spread by germs and not 'bad air'. A second edition of the essay, with evidence from the infected water supply in Soho, was published in 1855. Taken far more seriously than the first edition, it led to a detailed investigation of the public water supply in London and the eventual acceptance that cholera was transmitted through bad water and not bad air. John Snow rose to greater prominence, too, although he was already well known for his work on anaesthesia, personally administering chloroform to Queen Victoria during the births of her last two children in 1853 and 1857.

Now Londoners had an excuse for not drinking water, and began drinking even more beer and wine instead, knowing that the fermentation process would remove all traces of bacteria and so prevent the spread of water-transmitted disease. This is the reason the expression 'good health' is widely used by people having a drink together, because in London in the mid nineteenth century drinking alcohol really was a way of ensuring you didn't fall ill (or not from cholera, at any rate). Fittingly, Snow, despite being teetotal all his life, is commemorated by a public house bearing his name, built near the old water pump in Broad (now Broadwick) Street. The beer is fine; and, these days, so is the water.

The King's Head
THE NO BODY INN?

There are many pubs called the King's Head, all over Britain. The kings painted on their signs vary and most are a straightforward celebration of royalty. Those that feature Charles I, however, are rather more macabre, as in this case it is literally the king's head that is meant, unattached to the king's body.

Parliament had agonized over the execution of the king, knowing that while he was living he would remain the focus of constant uprisings, but that once dead he would become a martyr. It was difficult to find an executioner who was prepared to kill a monarch, however anonymously, and several refused, until an Irishman called Gunning accepted the job; in fact his name appears commemorated on a plaque in the King's Head pub in

Galway, Ireland. The execution was set for 30 January 1649, and Charles faced his death with courage, the vast crowd moaning as the executioner's axe fell. It was common practice for the head of a traitor to be held up and exhibited to the crowd with the words 'Behold the head of a traitor!' moments after the execution. Although Charles's head was exhibited, the words were not used, reflecting the popular regard in which he was still held.

In 1661, following his restoration to the throne, the king's son, Charles II, took his revenge on the man who had organized his father's death. The body of Oliver Cromwell was dug up (he'd died three years before) and his head placed on display at Westminster Hall, where it remained for a further twenty-four years as a grisly reminder to all those opposing the monarchy. This too is commemorated in another pub name – the **Cromwell's Head**. (See also THE DUKE'S HEAD.)

The Lamplighters
IN THE DARK NO ONE CAN HEAR YOU SCREAM . . .

It sounds a rather quaint name for a pub, but lamplighters were once a vital part of every urban community. In the days before electricity, they toured towns and cities every evening before dusk and, using a long pole with a burning wick at one end, they lit the lamps illuminating the streets. Lamplighters, who also served as watchmen, had the job of maintaining the lamps, too. They would clean the wicks, repairing and renewing them where necessary and making sure each had enough oil. Perhaps one reason that the Good Old Days are so called is because in the daytime things *were* good; it was at night that they were less enjoyable. Criminals took advantage of the darkness, while families huddled inside around the fire, telling each other ghost stories.

The invention of street lighting revolutionized people's lives as the day no longer needed to end at sunset. More than anything, this was, of course, good news for publicans as pubs could stay open much later. One good reason for calling your inn the Lamplighters was to remind your potential customers that you were open late (it's also why 'night' clubs are so called) and to point out that yours was in a well-patrolled part of town, as not all streets were lit.

By the nineteenth century, most oil lamps had been replaced by gas and, although initially these also needed to be lit by hand, a more efficient system was soon developed, enabling street lamps to be turned on automatically. By 1882, when Godalming, a small town near Guildford, became the first in the world to have electric street lighting, the days of the lamplighter were numbered and within a few years the familiar sight of the man with his pole lighting the lamps had become a thing of the past.

One of the first pubs in England to adopt the name is believed to be Lamplighter's Hall in Shirehampton, near Bristol, first recorded in 1768 when, on 17 December, it was advertised in the *Bristol Journal*: 'For let – the public house at Passage Leaze opposite [the village of] Pill, commonly known as Lamplighter's Hall.' In 1772 the property was advertised for sale by the estate of Joseph Swetnam, a prosperous businessman who at one time held the contracts to light and maintain the lamps of many Bristol parishes. He built the splendid house as a country residence but soon found the busy, and foul-smelling, River Avon did not suit his family and so the building was converted into a hotel, retaining the name Swetnam had given it, Lamplighter's Hall.

On 3 March 1793 American naval captain John Shaw went to dine at Lamplighter's Hall in the company of the notorious pirate Captain Henry Morgan. He noted: 'I cannot say I was highly entertained by the conversation, it being in a style I much disliked.' One hundred and fifty years later, the Welsh seaman, terror of the Spanish Main, was to inspire the name of one of the world's leading brands of rum – no doubt served at Lamplighters throughout the land.

The Lion and the Unicorn
AGE-OLD RIVALS FIGHT FOR THE CROWN

The lion and the unicorn are the symbols of the United Kingdom. In the same way that the Union Jack cleverly overlays England's St George cross with that of Scotland's St Andrew and of Ireland's St Patrick, the royal coat of arms is supported by the Scottish unicorn on one side and the English lion on the other (see THE WHITE LION). Of course, things aren't actually equal: the lion, not the unicorn, is generally depicted wearing the crown, but that harks back to a rather less stable time in Britain's history when a united kingdom was just wishful thinking.

The relationship between England and Scotland has traditionally been a tense one. The two countries were at constant odds with each other since long before the English invasion of 1296. But everything calmed down when James VI of Scotland became James I of England in 1603, uniting the two kingdoms under the Scottish Stuart dynasty. Unfortunately the Stuart dynasty didn't prove a particularly steady one and not one but two Stuart kings were sacked by Parliament and the people, who then turned to Europe for their new sovereign, in the shape of William of Orange from the Netherlands (see THE GEORGE).

The Scots were furious at the ousting of a Scottish royal family and consequently supported several rebellions against England led by various remaining members of the Stuart family. Unfortunately for them, both the Old Pretender and Bonnie Prince Charlie (see THE THREE LORDS) proved as unreliable a bet as their predecessors and the English army won a series of decisive victories. The Hanoverians were furious at what they saw as Scottish insubordination and went on a violent campaign of retribution, slaughtering those who still upheld the cause of the Stuarts and passing a series of laws deliberately designed to exterminate the Scottish way of life and culture. For instance, the wearing of kilts and tartans was punishable by seven years' imprisonment. Many pubs in Scotland were renamed the Lion and the Unicorn, ostensibly to show that the two countries were now united and were equals. Squashed and suppressed, the Scots were well aware, however, that the English were rather more equal than they were. It was still the lion that wore the crown.

The Lord Howard

THE MAN WHO SAVED ENGLAND FROM THE SPANISH

Cousin to Queen Elizabeth and all-round Renaissance man, Charles Howard (1536–1624), 1st Earl of Nottingham, was involved in every aspect of England's Golden Age, from sponsoring his own troupe of actors, the Admiral's Men, to suppressing the Earl of Essex's revolt and recommending the execution of Mary, Queen of Scots. But he is best known for his role in masterminding the trouncing of the Spanish Armada in 1587 (see also THE GOLDEN HIND).

His marriage proposals having been fobbed off by Elizabeth I for over twenty years, Philip II of Spain had finally decided to invade England. And he was doing it with the blessing of the Pope and the rest of Catholic Europe. Things did not look good for the English. The Spanish fleet was much larger (so large it took two full days for all the ships to leave Lisbon) and much better equipped than that of their English rivals. And the Armada was just one half of the invasion force: there was also an army of 30,000 in the Spanish Netherlands awaiting its arrival, the plan being to send the barges across the sea to England under cover of the warships. Were it not for a conveniently timed storm in the Channel that levelled the odds, history might have turned out very differently.

Once the Spanish ships had been sighted off the Cornish shore, a series of beacons were lighted along the south coast to carry the news to Howard and Sir Francis Drake at Plymouth, who set off with fifty-five ships to take on their larger and more powerful foe.

Drake carried out Howard's orders and is remembered as the man who defeated the Armada, but it was Howard who, as Lord High Admiral, was in overall command of naval operations at the time. Howard's strategy of hit-and-run attacks in the early stages, by ordering a policy of harassment rather than direct engagement with the Spanish, was initially unpopular until it proved successful.

Luckily for the English, the Spanish admiral, the Duke of Medina Sidonia, was too cautious, missing several opportunities to take the advantage while Howard and Drake whittled away at the Spanish fleet. At midnight on 28 July, the English set alight eight warships, filled with pitch, brimstone and gunpowder, and sent them towards the Armada, lying at anchor off the coast of Calais. Two fireships were intercepted by the Spanish and towed away, but the remainder continued towards the fleet, causing the ships to scatter in alarm. No Spanish vessels caught fire, but the defensive crescent formation that the Armada had been maintaining was now broken, and, with the wind in the wrong direction, the fleet could not recover its position. The English saw their moment, closed in for battle and won a glorious victory. For this, his name is commemorated on pub signs throughout Britain.

The Lord Kitchener
YOUR PUBLIC HOUSE NEEDS YOU!

You may not know who Lord Kitchener was but you'd certainly recognize him. He was the heavily moustachioed general pointing out of First World War recruitment posters, declaring: 'YOUR COUNTRY NEEDS YOU'. The picture was an accurate one: it had been his lifelong mission to be exactly what his country needed, but as a career soldier, that had entailed various changes along the way.

Horatio Kitchener was born in County Kerry, Ireland, on 24 June 1850, and his burgeoning military career was to take him to every corner of the British Empire. To the Middle East, where, appointed commander-in-chief of the Egyptian army after Britain had accidently gained control over the country, Kitchener led his forces into Khartoum to avenge the death of General Gordon (Queen Victoria's favourite soldier) and managed to re-occupy the Sudanese capital, becoming both the Governor of Sudan and a national idol back home in the process. To South Africa, where in 1900 he famously set about dealing with Boer resistance to British rule with characteristic ruthlessness, introducing the 'scorched earth' policy of burning Boer farms and establishing the use of concentration camps to house unruly South African citizens. (Yes, they were a British invention.) And then to India, where he was made commander-in-chief in 1902 and charged with improving the army out there (which he did).

For the following ten years, Kitchener continued to prove an outstanding military leader and politician and, on the outbreak of the First World War, he was reluctantly appointed to the post of secretary of state for war. With his long experience of military matters, his was the only voice of gloom in the cabinet. He predicted it would be a long war, warning that there would be huge casualties and that the conflict would be decided by Britain's last million men. Nonetheless, he rapidly set about his famous recruitment campaign, enlisting and training over three million new recruits, who soon became known as 'Kitchener's Army'.

In his recruitment of soldiers, planning of strategy and mobilization of industry, Kitchener was handicapped by bureaucracy and his own dislike of teamwork and delegation. Known to display more care and concern for his soldiers than any other British officer, he must have been horrified that so many of them were ordered from their trenches on pointless attacks, only to be cut to pieces by German machine-gun fire. Such was the wastefulness of these 'over the top' operations, many German machine-gunners began to refuse to shoot at the defenceless Tommies running across no man's land towards them. The German commanders resolved this problem of compassion among their troops by shooting any who refused to fire at the British, and so millions more soldiers continued to have their body parts scattered over a wide area by shells or landmines. Kitchener's public concern for the British soldiers on the front line ensured his popularity with the public but began to earn him enemies within the cabinet, some of whom hoped he would take charge of Gallipoli and the Near East following a tour of inspection there in 1915, relocating to the region and out of the public eye.

On 5 June 1916 Kitchener was on a diplomatic mission to Russia aboard HMS *Hampshire* when the ship hit a mine, close to the Orkneys, and sank with the loss of 643 lives, Lord Kitchener among them. His great fame and popularity, coupled with his sudden death, immediately bred a host of conspiracy theories claiming either murder or assassination by the British government, German spies or angry Boers. The fact his body has never been recovered leaves such questions for ever unanswered. But Lord Kitchener will always be remembered as, following the war, the British public immediately began renaming streets, parks, schools, pubs and hotels in his honour.

The Lord Palmerston

THE POPULAR GUNBOAT DIPLOMAT WHO FAILED TO AMUSE QUEEN VICTORIA

Henry John Temple (1784–1865) was born just five years before the revolution that, in France, led to noble families like his own being locked up and taken to the guillotine. Henry, aged just eighteen, became 3rd Viscount Palmerston in April 1802, the year before Napoleon Bonaparte led his newly formed French republic into war against his European neighbours. War-hungry Palmerston became an MP in 1807 and was then given the post of Junior Lord of the Admiralty, thanks to a little smoothing of the way for him by friends of his late father, such was the way politics worked in the good old days. Brought up in such uncertain times, he was to remain obsessed with pre-emptively attacking Britain's enemies for the rest of his long career

As war in Europe raged on, despite great British victories like the one at Trafalgar (see THE ADMIRAL COLLINGWOOD and THE NELSON), Palmerston delivered his debut speech to the House of Commons, in which he defended the expedition to Copenhagen by the Royal Navy, pointing out that Napoleon sought to control the Danish port as it was vital to his overall campaign.

Having impressed all who heard him, Palmerston was offered the position of Chancellor of the Exchequer in 1809 by the new prime minister, Spencer Perceval (1762–1812), who was to find lasting fame by becoming the only British prime minister ever to be assassinated when he was gunned down in the lobby of the House of Commons by John Bellingham, a man who blamed the government for his personal financial crisis. (Don't all rush at once, ladies and gentlemen; form an orderly queue!)

Palmerston instead took the post of secretary of war, with specific responsibilities for the finances of the military forces, a position he held, on and off, for twenty years. From 1830 he became foreign secretary, his abrasive style and uncompromising method of dealing with foreign powers leading to the nickname 'Lord Pumice Stone' and to the phrase 'gunboat diplomacy'. The latter expression arose as a result of what was referred to as the Don Pacifico Incident. In 1850, when British subject David Pacifico was injured in Athens, and the Greeks had refused to compensate him, Palmerston responded by sending a fleet of Royal Navy gunboats to blockade the Greek port of Piraeus until they did.

Defending his actions in a five-hour speech at the House

of Commons, Palmerston insisted that any British subject anywhere in the world had a right to be protected by his government against injustice. Unsurprisingly, the speech made him the most popular politician in the country – popular with the people, that is, not the other politicians, who were horrified by his trigger-happy approach to foreign policy. And after much manoeuvring by his rivals, in 1852 he was made home secretary, and thus was powerless to prevent the Crimean War (see THE ALMA) breaking out, which some historians believe he might have been able to stop. Despite arguing for action against the Russians at various key points, he was overruled.

But it was not a successful war and after the disastrous Charge of the Light Brigade led to public outrage, Palmerston was finally summoned to Buckingham Palace by Queen Victoria, on 4 February 1855, and invited to form a government, despite her obvious personal dislike for the man. The queen later wrote in her private diary: 'We had, God knows, terrible trouble with him about Foreign Affairs. Still, as prime minister he managed affairs at home very well and behaved very well to me. But I never liked him.'

The problem was that Victoria and her husband, Prince Albert, were closely related to many of the ruling royal families of Europe and they found Palmerston's uncompromising approach embarrassing, to say the least. Imagine the scene at one of her famous family get-togethers at Osbourne House on the Isle of Wight: 'Nice lunch, cousin Victoria, but could you ask your ghastly prime minister to get his gunboats out of my harbour?' But the more he irritated the ruling classes, the more wildly popular he became with the British people, suspicious as ever about all activities of Johnny Foreigner.

Palmerston may have been popular with the working classes, but he cared little about them, even resigning when a bill was proposed to give them the vote. He later wrote to William Gladstone: 'if we open the door to the working class, the number who may come in may be excessive, and swamp the classes above them. The result would arise not merely from the number let in, but also from the fact that the influx discourages the classes above them from voting at all.'

Pubs named after him sprang up all over Britain, unimpeded by the fact that, in a time of strong moral values, Palmerston was also notorious for his womanizing. When he was caught trying to seduce one of her ladies-in-waiting at Windsor Castle, a furious Victoria wanted him fired, but Lord Melbourne persuaded her to change her mind. This narrow escape didn't change the behaviour of the man *The Times* called Lord Cupid. He was even cited as the co-respondent in a divorce case at the age of seventy-nine.

Within a year of being appointed prime minister, Palmerston had signed a peace treaty ending the Crimean War and allowing British soldiers to return home. His efforts earned him the Order of the Garter (see THE STAR AND GARTER), and although his term of office ended on 19 February 1858, he was re-elected for a second term on 12 June 1859, a position he held for over six years, steering Britain through a period in which it had the most powerful empire on earth.

When he won another general election in July 1865, many confidently expected that he would continue in his role for several more years, so there was huge shock when he died suddenly, in a cabinet meeting, two days before his eighty-first birthday, on 18 October 1865. He died in harness, his final words being: 'Right that's Article 98; now go on to the rest.' And he was rewarded by being only the fourth Briton in history outside the royal family to be honoured with a state funeral, the others being Sir Isaac Newton, the Duke of Wellington (see THE IRON DUKE) and Lord Horatio NELSON. His name lives on in the many pubs and bars called the **Palmerston** or the Lord Palmerston.

Lord's Tavern
(St John's Wood, London)

THE COMMONER WHO CHANGED THE FACE OF THE
ULTIMATE GENTLEMAN'S SPORT

Lord's Tavern (or Lord's Tavern Bar & Brasserie, as it's called these days), the famous bar on St John's Wood Road, London, has a long association with English cricket. It is often assumed that both the ground and tavern were inspired by the elitism of the game, either by a single lord or a collection of lords who may have grouped together many years past to form a cricket club. But the name provides the clue: Lord's Tavern and Lord's Cricket-Ground, not *the* Lord's. They aren't named after a generic nobleman but after a specific, untitled and highly unusual man.

Thomas Lord was born in 1755, the son of a Jacobite rebel (see THE THREE LORDS). Impoverished after the government had seized his land in punishment, his father had to work as a labourer. So from an early age Thomas learned the lesson that you should follow your dream only as long as you're not out of pocket. Luckily Lord's dream was a simpler one than his father's: to play cricket.

As an adult he moved to London and found work at the White Conduit Club in Islington. The WCC was formed in London in about 1780, primarily as a gentlemen's club whose activities centred chiefly upon the game of cricket, a sport that had become well established in London and the south-east of England. Large sums of money were wagered on the outcome of matches and thus winning was hugely important. While the WCC initially only allowed members of a certain status in society, they also employed professional players with a talent for cricket. Thomas Lord, a well-respected bowler, albeit a commoner from a working-class family, was one of the professionals the nobility took on to raise the quality of their game.

In addition to Lord's ability on the field, he was also soon recognized for his business acumen and within a few years was effectively running the club. But while the club was exclusive, White Conduit Fields was an open area allowing members of the public, including the rowdier elements, to watch the matches and to voice their opinions on the play and the players, which did not amuse the gentlemen cricketers at all. In 1785 two of the WCC's leading figures, the Earl of Winchilsea and Colonel Charles Lennox (later the Duke of Richmond), approached Lord with the idea of forming a brand-new cricket club where the gentry did not have to share their facilities with riff-raff. Offering Lord a financial indemnity against any losses he might incur with the new venture, the two men encouraged the bowler to move fast and in 1787 Lord's Cricket Ground was opened on land leased from the Portland estate in Marylebone.

So the Marylebone Cricket Club was formed, staging its first match on 31 May 1787. A year later, it laid down a set of laws, requiring the wickets to be pitched twenty-two yards apart and detailing how players should be placed. Its laws were adopted throughout the game, and MCC today remains the custodian and arbiter of laws relating to the playing of cricket around the world.

After a short stay at Marylebone Bank, Regent's Park, between 1811 and 1813, Lord's moved to a new rural ground – previously the site of a duck pond – in St John's Wood in 1814 but kept the name Marylebone. The ground was soon a major success and attracted hordes of players and spectators, forcing Lord to build a pavilion and refreshment stalls (in those days refreshments were almost always alcoholic). It remains the MCC's home to this day and it also houses the oldest sporting museum on the planet. The original urn holding the Ashes trophy played for biennually in a series of test matches between England and Australia has been housed at Lord's since 1882 and never leaves the museum. (The winner of the matches is presented with a replica.)

Despite his noble clients' promises to underwrite expenses, cricket alone was not enough to keep Lord's ground afloat and he had to hold all kinds of extra events there, from football matches to balloon ascents, to make ends meet. At the age of seventy, an exhausted Thomas Lord retired from cricket, business and London life, selling his cricket ground to a Bank of England director and respected batsman, William Ward, for £5,000. He died two years later at West Meon in Hampshire and is buried there, in the graveyard of St John's Church. The church itself is just along the lane from another public house called after the man who gave his name to the most famous cricketing ground, and tavern, in the world.

In 1868, to cater for the growing number of cricket lovers attending matches at Lord's, the architect Edward Paraire, who specialized in designing pubs and churches, replaced the refreshments stand with a proper building. Called Lord's Tavern, it was originally located within the ground and had an elegant wrought-iron balcony overlooking the pitch. It was later moved just outside the main gates, along the St John's Wood Road, but remains one of the most famous pubs in the world, visited by cricketing fans of all nationalities come to London to see their team play.

The Maltings

PREPARING THE VITAL INGREDIENT FOR THE VITAL
INGREDIENT OF EVERY PUB

The Maltings is a pub name that refers to the making of every pub's most popular drink, malted grain being the vital ingredient in beer. Malting – thought to have evolved from the word 'melt' – consists of the controlled germination and drying of cereal grains, generally barley (see THE JOHN BARLEYCORN and THE WHEATSHEAF). In a process that goes back over four thousand years, grain is spread out, traditionally over a stone floor, and left to soak in water for anywhere between five and ten days until it begins to sprout. As soon as it does, it is then quickly dried in kilns to prevent further germination, and then the grain is ready to be used.

The first step of brewing is to add hot water to the malted grain, which then ferments as the starches in the grain change into sugars. This increasingly alcoholic liquid provides the basis for beer.

The maltings, another term for the 'malting floor' or the 'malt house', would in some cases have been vast warehouses. Falling into disuse over the years, many have since been converted into pubs, hotels, theatres and even shopping centres, often still bearing the name the Maltings or the **Malt House**, to show their past connection with the brewing industry.

The Marquis of Granby

THE BALD BULLY WITH A SOFT HEART COMMEMORATED BY
PUBS ALL OVER BRITAIN

The Marquess of Granby (usually rendered 'Marquis' in
the pub name) is the traditional title of the eldest son of the
Duke of Rutland, so there have been many Marquesses of
Granby, but the ubiquitous pub of that name is called after
just one, another fondly remembered, flawed British hero.

Dismissed by George II as a drunkard and bully, John
Manners, Marquess of Granby, only came into his own
during the Seven Years' War (1756–63), in which he was
appointed Colonel of the Royal Horse Guards, later promoted to lieutenant general. All the major European
powers of the time were involved in the fighting, 1.5 million soldiers dying in a conflict later described by Winston Churchill as the 'real first world war'. The marquess
may have liked a drink (or three) but he wasn't lacking in
courage. On 31 July 1760 he led the cavalry on a daring
charge against the French at the Battle of Warburg, capturing nearly 2,000 enemy soldiers and many much
needed guns. Granby had been bald since his early twen-
ties but in a time where most people wore wigs, he saw
no need to. During the charge he lost his hat but he kept
charging at the enemy, giving rise, it is believed, to the
expression 'going at it bald headed'.

Yet despite being such an inspiring soldier that one of
his opponents even commissioned a portrait of him after
the war, the marquess lacked administrative skills and
was often criticized by his fellow officers for the leniency
he showed his men. This was seen as weakness at the

time, conducive to a lack of discipline among the rank and file, which some thought made him unfit for command. The public loved him, however, and his popularity is reflected in a contemporary painting by Edward Penny, *The Marquess of Granby Relieving a Sick Soldier*, showing the general's compassion for his fellow man rather than portraying him, more conventionally, as the conquering hero. Prints of the picture were displayed proudly in many Georgian homes.

After the war was over, Granby turned his attention to politics, at which he proved somewhat less successful. His hot temper and hard drinking were less suited to diplomacy and led to a series of disastrous mistakes. But he always remained available to any man who had served under his command during the war. It has been reported that on many occasions he helped members of his old regiment establish themselves as innkeepers, many of whom would honour their former general by calling their establishments after him.

Molly Maguires
HOW IRELAND'S TRANVESTITE TERRORISTS INFILTRATED AMERICA

There are Molly Maguires pubs and restaurants all along the east coast of America and throughout Britain, especially in Scotland and Ireland. Molly Maguire sounds like a completely innocuous generic female name, but that's what it supposed to sound like. The story behind the name is much darker.

Ireland in the late eighteenth century and throughout

the nineteenth was full of secret societies with names such as Whiteboys or Peep O'Day Boys; in Donegal it was the Molly Maguires. Bound to secrecy, they acted to protect the interests of the smallholders and peasants whose land was being seized by unsympathetic landlords. Their resistance often took the form of destructive acts such as breaking fences, ploughing up pasture land and killing, maiming or driving off livestock. According to historian Kevin Kenny in his book *Making Sense of the Molly Maguires*, the Mollies believed that they were carrying out 'a just law of their own in opposition to the inequities of landlord law, the police and court system, and the transgressions of land-grabbers'.

Local businesses were threatened or attacked if their prices were too high, while landlords' agents could be beaten or even killed. New tenants occupying land from which the previous tenants had been evicted were also targeted. Leaders of the Molly Maguires were known to have dressed as women in order to surprise their adversaries. They might enter a shop, for instance, and demand groceries or other supplies. If their demands were not met, they would take what they wanted, threatening reprisals if their actions were reported. This was a world many Irish immigrants to America were more than happy to have left behind.

In the mid nineteenth century, industry was growing quickly in America along the east coast. The infrastructure was supported almost entirely by migrant Irish workers, who flooded into the New World looking for a new life. Sadly, for many of them this turned out to be just as bad as the one they had left behind.

Most workers and their families were required to live in

company-owned houses in company-owned towns, and were forced to buy everything they needed from company-owned stores that often overcharged for their goods. Working conditions for the immigrant labour force in the coal mines and on the railways were so bad that hundreds were killed and thousands seriously injured in accidents that could have been easily avoided. The families of those who were no longer able to work due to death or injury were often forced out of their houses to beg or starve. Enormous resentment started to grow and action began to be taken.

In 1868 John Siney, an Irishman with experience of working in the English mines, was inspired to form the Workingmen's Benevolent Association (WBA) to demand an improvement in both pay and working conditions. The following year, on 6 September 1869, 110 coal miners died in a fire at the Avondale Mine in Pennsylvania. As the charred bodies of the miners were brought up, Siney climbed on to a wagon and shouted to the crowds below: 'Men, if you must die with your boots on, die for your families, your homes, your country, but do not consent to die, like rats in a trap, for those who have no more interest in you than the pick you use to dig with.' In an instant, thousands of miners had joined Siney's union.

Plutocrats love profit and they hate unions. The company owners responded by hiring the Pinkerton Agency, the famous detective agency whose use of an eye as their company logo led to the expression 'private eye' becoming synonymous with the private detective. They sent an agent to infiltrate the newly formed union, one James McParlan, an Irish immigrant himself. He joined the WBA and, in the process of investigating the union, discovered that many unionists were also members of the Molly Maguires, responsible for much of the violence being committed at that time against the mine and its owners.

Becoming suspicious of McParlan, the Molly Maguires in turn started to investigate him, but the detective was tipped off and fled the area, taking with him evidence about the murders of over fifty mine managers across the region. A well-publicized show trial followed in 1876 and McParlan was the star witness. Many believed that the evidence had been fabricated and that none of the accused men received a fair trial. Whether that is true or not, the resulting execution on 21 June 1877 of twenty members of the Molly Maguires instantly turned them into martyrs and the name has been associated ever since with the struggle against labour injustice.

While there is no doubt that it is the controversial freedom fighters after which the eponymous pubs and hotels are named, it's not known who the real Molly Maguire was, although there are various theories. Some historians insist the name evolved from the practice of the men disguising themselves as women when committing crimes. Others believe Molly owned the drinking den where the members met and planned their secret operations, or that Molly herself was a member and bravely led the men on night-time raids. But the story I prefer is that the original Molly Maguire was a wife and mother who was turned out of her house after her husband had been killed in an accident. A group of peasants, calling themselves after her, were finally inspired to take decisive action when poor Molly died in poverty before they could help her.

Molly Malone's
THE TRUE STORY OF THE TROLLOP WITH THE SCALLOPS

Hundreds of Irish pubs worldwide are called Molly Malone's. But let's make one thing clear: there's no such thing as an Irish pub outside of Ireland. Imagine the disappointment I felt on my first visit to Dubai only to find the bar right next to the beautiful hotel I was staying in was called Molly Malone's. At least I could sink a cold beer in there, but it felt like Woking during a heatwave. There are lots of pubs with an Irish name, painted green and with the Guinness logo prominently displayed, but that doesn't make them Irish; they are just pubs with an Irish theme. The only proper Irish pubs are in Ireland. However, I digress. Who was Molly Malone and why is her name so popular as a choice of (Irish) pub name?

'The Ballad of Molly Malone' is one of the best-known songs in Ireland and the unofficial anthem of the Irish capital, Dublin. While it's not known when the song was originally written, it was first published in 1883 in Cambridge, Massachusetts. In the song Molly is portrayed as the pretty young daughter of a Dublin fishmonger who used to wheel her father's market barrow up and down Grafton Street, calling out 'Cockles and mussels' to advertise her wares.

> In Dublin's fair city,
> Where the girls are so pretty,
> I first set my eyes on sweet Molly Malone,
> As she wheeled her wheelbarrow,

Through streets broad and narrow,
Crying, 'Cockles and mussels alive, alive, oh!'

She was a fishmonger,
And sure 'twas no wonder,
For so were her father and mother before,
And they each wheeled their barrow,
Through streets broad and narrow,
Crying, 'Cockles and mussels alive, alive, oh!'

She died of a fever,
And no one could save her,
And that was the end of sweet Molly Malone.
Now her ghost wheels her barrow,
Through streets broad and narrow,
Crying, 'Cockles and mussels alive, alive, oh!'

One school of thought suggests that Molly was a prostitute by night, while another argues she was the only lady street hawker of the time who wasn't. 'Cockles and mussels' was a common fishmonger's cry of the time, but as it was also used as slang for the female private parts, Molly could have been selling her own 'wares' at the same time. Women involved in the fish trade were notorious for their loose morals and foul mouths – hence the expression 'swearing like a fishwife' and London's famous fish market, Billingsgate, becoming a byword for crude and vulgar language. The fever that Molly dies from is deliberately unspecified; it could have easily been some kind of sexually transmitted disease. But you can choose for yourselves which version you want to believe.

It is suggested that Molly was a real woman who lived some time in the seventeenth century, but there is no evidence for this. Molly was a common nickname for Mary or Margaret (see also THE MOLLY PITCHER). And while many Molly Malones would have been born in Dublin over the centuries, there is nothing to connect any of them with the events in the song. Nevertheless, in 1988 the Dublin Millennium Commission endorsed claims concerning a Molly Malone who died on 13 June 1699, and proclaimed 13 June to be Molly Malone Day.

A year earlier, in 1987, a statue of Molly was unveiled at the top end of Grafton Street, to mark the city's millennium, portraying her as a beautiful young lady wearing an extremely low-cut seventeenth-century gown. This was justified by city officials on the grounds of breast-feeding in public being common in Dublin during Molly's day: 'breasts popped out all over the place'. The now famous statue is known locally as the 'trollop with the scallops', the 'dish with the fish', or the 'tart with the cart', and Molly has become something of a tourist attraction over the years – one of the most photographed in the entire city. Now, why doesn't that surprise me?

The Molly Pitcher
THE ORIGINAL CANNONBALL RUN ...

America is littered with bars and taverns called the Molly Pitcher, which at first glance appears to be the perfect name for yet another chain of Irish theme pubs. But there is no connection between the Molly Pitcher Highway leading to the Maryland state line and the **Molly Pitcher**

Inn on the New Jersey Turnpike, or the Molly Pitcher Waffle House in Chambersburg, Pennsylvania, and there is nothing Irish about any of them. Indeed, they're not named after an Irish girl but an American one.

Molly Pitcher was a generic name given to women who participated in the War of Independence (1775–83), fought against the British (see also THE ADDISON ARMS and THE JOHN PAUL JONES). Molly was a nickname for Mary or Margaret (see also MOLLY MALONE'S), both very common names. The surname 'Pitcher' refers to the way in which these women bravely carried pitchers of water and tended to wounded soldiers on the battlefield, often carrying ammunition to the front line and, in some cases, even manning the guns. Molly Pitchers were wives, sweethearts and even mothers (presumably in some cases all three) and their back-up was crucial to the eventual success of the American cause.

Although 'Molly Pitcher' rapidly became synonymous with all the women helping on the battlefield, it appears there was one woman who inspired the nickname. Mary Ludwig was born on 13 October 1754 near Philadelphia in the state of Pennsylvania. She grew up and married a young barber called William Hays, who, in 1775, at the start of the American War of Independence, volunteered for the first Pennsylvania Artillery Regiment, training as a gunner. On 28 June 1778 the regiment, under the overall command of George Washington, engaged the British in New Jersey in what became known as the Battle of Monmouth. What seems unthinkable today is how the great and the good of American society rushed with enormous excitement to take up prime positions close to the battlefield in order to witness the unfolding events for themselves. Wives, mothers and other family members of the soldiers also travelled with the army, hoping for a ringside seat.

As expected, when the battle began, many were unprepared for the horrors of war and were sickened to witness friends and family being cut to pieces by the British artillery. The sight of the soldiers lying dying and wounded, scattered around the battlefield in the hundred-degree heat, was too much for one young woman to bear. Grabbing a pitcher of water, Mary rushed out to tend to the troops, her actions inspiring others to brave the war zone and carry water, bandages and other supplies to their fallen friends. Some say that Mary went even further and manned her husband's gun after he too became a casualty.

Joseph Plumb Martin (1760–1850), a soldier whose war memoirs were later published, noted of Mary:

While in the act of reaching a cartridge and having one of her feet as far before the other as she could step, a cannon shot from the enemy passed directly between her legs without doing any damage other than carrying away all the lower part of her petticoat. Looking at it with apparent unconcern, she observed that it was lucky it did not pass a little higher, for in that case it might have carried away something else, and ended her and her occupation.

Whether that was what she really said, Mary clearly had great presence of mind. Indeed, after the battle she was presented to George Washington, who was so impressed with her courage that he made her a non-commissioned officer, after which she became known by the affectionate title of 'Sergeant Molly'.

For many years after the war, the standard artillery regimental toast was: 'Drunk in a beverage richer and stronger than was poured that day from Molly Pitcher's pitcher.' It's easy to see why Molly Pitcher has become such a popular name for pubs and bars, offering, as they do, a welcome cooling drink to the tired, weary and battle-scarred, just as Mary did.

After her husband's death in about 1789, Mary married George McCauley and became known as Mary Hays McCauley, although it is by her nickname of Molly Pitcher that she will for ever be remembered. Mary died on 22 January 1832 and is buried next to the Molly Pitcher Monument in Carlisle, Pennsylvania. She sounds like my sister to me: you wouldn't want to confront her on a battlefield either.

The Nag's Head
A TRICK BY PIRATES, HORSE FOR HIRE OR WOMAN TO AVOID?

The Nag's Head sounds like a straightforward enough pub name, but there are three very different theories about its origin. The first can be traced to the golden age of piracy in the Caribbean (from about 1650 to the 1720s). Returning home laden with booty, a pirate ship would wait out at sea under cover of darkness until a sign from the shore indicated that it was safe to land. Meanwhile, on the shore an accomplice would fix a lantern around the neck of an old horse and walk the 'nag' along the cliff top or highest point as a signal to the ship that the coast was clear. The sight of the bobbing lantern, known as the 'nag's head', would have been welcomed by returning pirates as a sign that their long, perilous voyage was over and the drinking could, at last, begin. The coastal town of Nags Head, a resort in Dare County, North Carolina, is built on land characterized by high sand dunes that can be seen far out to sea. Its name stands as a proud reflection of the old pirating practice.

The second theory is more directly related to pubs, and to pub signs in particular. The word 'nag', for a horse, is believed to have evolved from the Dutch word *negge*, meaning a small horse or pony. The word is usually applied to a horse that is old or in poor health but it originally meant a horse for riding, as opposed to one for pulling a cart or carriage. Travellers often needed to change horses in the course of a long trip and could hire them from country inns and taverns. Such a place with a horse for hire is likely to have displayed a horse's (nag's) head on a sign outside, informing travellers they could change their mounts there. The expression 'straight from the horse's mouth' comes from a horse's age being easily determined by looking at its teeth. If you were considering hiring a horse and needed to confirm that it wasn't likely to fall down dead a mile down the road, rather than relying on the say-so of the possibly dodgy innkeeper, you would open the animal's mouth and check the teeth. Hence you could tell at once, straight from the horse's mouth, whether the animal was in good enough shape.

The third, and my favourite, explanation comes from the other meaning of 'nag', someone who constantly carps and criticizes. Traditionally a pub's clientele was mostly male, the men often using the inn as a refuge from the busy tongues of their wives (see also THE QUIET WOMAN). More than one Nag's Head pub sign has been jokingly daubed with a macabre painting of a woman's head, her mouth still open in complaint, to show its customers (and their wives) that nagging *really* isn't welcome there.

The Nell Gwyn

ENGLAND'S FAVOURITE ROYAL MISTRESS

If anyone was going to epitomize the spirit of Restoration England it was Nell Gwyn (1650–87). Deserted by her father, a Royalist captain, Nell worked from an early age, selling oranges and lemons to theatre audiences in Drury Lane, and soon became known for her humour, infectious high spirits and occasional misbehaviour.

By 1665 Nell had been encouraged by her first lover, the forty-year-old actor Charles Hart, to appear on stage in

John Dryden's *Indian Emperor*, but it was her role in the comedies of James Howard the following year that drew the attention of London society with Samuel Pepys commenting 'pretty, witty Nell' on the first occasion he saw her. Pepys recorded her wit on another occasion, following a petty argument between the young actress and a friend:

> Here Mrs Pierce tells me . . . that Nelly and Beck Marshall, falling out the other day, the latter called the other my Lord Buckhurst's whore. Nell answered then, 'I was but one man's whore, though I was brought up in a bawdy-house . . . and you are whore to three or four, though a Presbyter's praying daughter!'

While it's not clear exactly when Nell and Charles II became lovers, it is recorded that the sixteen-year-old and her mother followed the king and his court to Oxford to avoid the Great Plague, which was then sweeping London. While still a teenager, she fell pregnant with the king's seventh son. The baby, the future Duke of St Albans, was born soon after her twentieth birthday. This established Nell as the king's principal lover, but, by then, her growing popularity as an actress and dancer was also endearing her to the public.

Uninterested in status (Nell never fought for the king's attention among his other courtesans), the young actress embodied the spirit of the new England emerging from Cromwell's austere Puritan rule and was seen to be a true child of the modern, more liberated times. She also remained faithful to the king throughout his life and to his memory beyond it. On his deathbed Charles desperately appealed to his younger brother, and heir, James II: 'Let not poor Nelly starve.' James honoured his brother's wishes and Nell was generously provided for by the crown until her death in London in November 1687.

The Nelson

THE FLAWED HERO WHO WAS PLACED ON A PEDESTAL BY THE ESTABLISHMENT

The statue of Nelson that stands, flanked by stone lions, in the centre of Trafalgar Square is an interesting testament to how the Victorians commemorated their war heroes. The column itself is so tall that it is hard to make out the details of the figure. Far too grand and imposing, Nelson's Column conveys little of the humanity that made the man so special and popular with the general public, demonstrating, quite literally, the danger of placing individuals on high pedestals

– the truth quickly becomes obscured. Like so many British heroes immortalized in the names of pubs, Horatio Nelson (1758–1805) was in reality a highly complicated figure who seemed to have taken the adage 'all's fair in love and war' as his motto. His enormous courage and daring helped saved Britain from Napoleon, but this was offset by a flamboyant love life and complete disregard for public opinion, which caused huge scandal.

When Nelson was twelve, his uncle Maurice, sensing his ability, persuaded him to go to sea. Although plagued with a seasickness, which never left him, Nelson didn't allow that to hold him back. Like his hero Francis Drake and his best friend Cuthbert Collingwood (see THE ADMIRAL COLLINGWOOD and THE GOLDEN HIND), he rapidly climbed the ranks, rising to the position of captain by the age of twenty. During those early years, as well as becoming popular for the emphasis he placed on the health and safety of his men, Nelson earned a reputation for his ambitious naval tactics and personal bravery. But once the American War of Independence was over, in 1783, the young captain found himself unemployed and so returned with his new wife, Fanny, to Norfolk, where he spent several frustrating years battling illness and contemplating his future.

But his fortunes changed with the outbreak of the French Revolutionary Wars in 1792. The Royal Navy moved quickly to re-establish their naval power by recalling many talented young commanders, including Horatio Nelson, who was immediately posted to the Mediterranean. There he took part in several minor skirmishes against the French, before capturing the island of Corsica, Napoleon's birthplace. It was during the Battle of Calvi, in 1794, that Nelson lost the sight of his right eye after a

French cannonball hit a sandbag, sending a shower of tiny stones into his face. Although Nelson is often depicted in pub signs as wearing an eye patch, that's part of the Nelson myth; he actually never did so, as his eyeball sustained no obvious damage and there was no disfigurement to hide apart from as small scar on his forehead.

Three years later, in 1797, Nelson shot to fame at the Battle of Cape St Vincent when the English fleet, led by Admiral Sir John Jervis on his flagship HMS *Victory*, defeated a much larger Spanish fleet off the Portuguese coast. Despite disobeying orders, breaking away from the line of warships to engage with the Spanish, Nelson contributed directly to the victory by capturing two enemy vessels out of the four that surrendered. Misfortune then followed at the Battle of Santa Cruz de Tenerife later that year, when, during the early exchanges, he was hit in the arm by a musket ball, shattering the bones in several places. Such was his devotion to duty, however, that Nelson ordered the ship's surgeon to remove the damaged arm and was back in command within the hour, issuing new orders to his captains. The following year saw victory again: Nelson led the fleet against French forces at the Battle of the Nile, obliterating the fleet that was anchored at Alexandria and isolating Napoleon's troops in Egypt.

Sailing to Naples after the battle, Nelson stayed with Sir William Hamilton, the British envoy, and his beautiful and much younger wife, Emma, daughter of a Cheshire blacksmith and a former courtesan. It was her hero-worship of her illustrious guest that laid the foundation for their famous love affair. Nelson was by no means handsome – his adventures had prematurely aged him: he had lost an eye, an arm and most of his teeth, and he was afflicted by coughing spells. Despite this, Emma Hamilton reportedly flung herself upon him in admiration, calling out, 'Oh God, is it possible?', before fainting against him.

Their relationship caused a scandal both in the Mediterranean and later in London, when Nelson returned to England in the company of the Hamiltons. Nelson was given a hero's welcome; he attended court and attended a number of banquets and balls held in his honour. Madly in love with Emma, he grew increasingly cold towards Fanny, hating even to be in the same room as her. When she issued an ultimatum, asking him to choose between herself and Emma, Nelson chose Emma.

His affair was now public knowledge; and Emma gave birth to their daughter, Horatia, on 31 January 1801. By the autumn Nelson had bought a small ramshackle house on the outskirts of Wimbledon. There he lived openly with Emma, Sir William and Emma's mother, in a ménage à quatre that fascinated the public. The newspapers reported on their every move, looking to Emma to set fashions in dress, home decoration and even dinner party menus.

Despite his disabilities, Nelson remained in active service (the navy was desperate to separate its hero from his scandalous lifestyle) and later that year he found himself in action at Copenhagen, where he won another victory, this time over the Danes. A well-known phrase in English owes its existence to Nelson's actions during the battle. Nelson's boss and the commander of the British fleet, Admiral Sir Hyde Parker, was watching Nelson's attack on the Danish navy. At one point, however, Parker felt that the fleet was taking unnecessary risks and bearing unacceptable losses, so he ordered Nelson, via a series of flags, to disengage.

When Nelson's officers pointed out the message, he deliberately raised a telescope to his blind eye and replied: 'I do not see any signal.' Nelson then returned his attention to the battle and soundly defeated the Danes. On his return to London, he was made a viscount and put in overall command of the Channel fleet, which was to lead to his defining moment at the Battle of Trafalgar in 1805. The newspapers reported that the famous sailor had 'turned his blind eye' to his orders and won a resounding victory, an expression still in use today.

However, it was four years later, at Trafalgar, off the coast of Spain, that Nelson found lasting fame, leading his fleet into the battle that remains for ever associated with his name, along with the immortal phrase 'England expects that every man will do his duty'. Very early in the battle, he was struck by a bullet that tore through his spine, and he died three hours later. His old friend Collingwood valiantly took over command and led the fleet to victory, but all the acclaim was for Nelson. Preserved in a barrel of brandy lashed to the mast of HMS *Victory*, the body of Vice Admiral Horatio Nelson, 1st Viscount Nelson, 1st Duke of Bronté, KB was brought home for a lavish state funeral and laid to rest at St Paul's Cathedral in London.

Following his death, the government was already trying to recreate him in the mould of the hero they wanted him to be, and his dying wish that Emma Hamilton should be looked after was ignored, to such an extent that she was even denied permission to attend his funeral and all money and titles were awarded to his legitimate family. NELL GWYN would have been furious at Emma Hamilton's mistreatment. The famous statue erected in 1843 at the top of its 151-foot column presents the official, expurgated version of England's greatest sailor. But it is the scarred, human Nelson that people took to their hearts and whose image adorns pub signs throughout the English-speaking world.

The Oddfellows' Arms
THE ANCIENT SOCIETY WITH A BIG INFLUENCE ON MODERN INSTITUTIONS

Fraternal, mutual or friendly societies (see also THE FOR-ESTERS' ARMS) can be traced back as far as 586 BC when the Babylonians conquered the House of David and ransacked Jerusalem, killing many Israelites and deporting the rest into captivity. This, by the way, was when all the trouble started between Jerusalem's Jewish inhabitants and their Arab neighbours: Nebuchadnezzar II, the ruler of Babylon, has a lot to answer for.

Those Israelites who managed to escape formed into a brotherhood affording mutual security and support. After thirty years in exile, the Israelites were invited by the Persian King Cyrus the Great to return and rebuild Jerusalem and their temples, but the mutual societies continued to thrive even in this period of peace. Their bonds grew so strong, they easily survived the fall of Jerusalem to the Roman Empire in AD 70. Those spared slaughter were taken to Rome by Emperor Vespasian and most would later serve in the Roman army all over Europe, taking with them the secret codes and customs of their brotherhood, and ensuring that any two members could privately identify themselves anywhere they met.

This concept of mutual support first surfaced in Britain

around AD 100 among Roman soldiers who made regular financial donations into a 'pot' that was held by the most senior centurion. If any of their number was forced to retire due to injury, a donation would be made from the pot to help him along his way. In other Roman-held European countries, particularly France and Spain, the fellowships spread throughout the rank and file in various forms and were firmly established by the time the great empire fell during the fifth century.

Seven hundred years later, the first formal order is believed to have been established in the City of London by Jean de Neuville and five other French knights. But the evolution of the Oddfellows in Britain can be more clearly traced in the development of the guilds of craftsmen, which began taking shape in London during the thirteenth century. The guilds changed the lives of working men as, for the first time, they now had strength in numbers and were able to influence an economy previously dominated by the monarch and the nobility.

The master guilds grew powerful and wealthy as tradesmen looked after each other and the families of those out of work or no longer capable of working, in an early form of trade unionization; but during the fifteenth century they began protecting their power and wealth by restricting membership, effectively establishing the sort of elite society they had originally banded together to oppose.

In opposition to this move, the less experienced or newly qualified tradesmen decided to form their own fellowships and rival guilds. However, they found themselves short on numbers as many smaller towns simply didn't have enough members of the same trade who were not already part of an established guild to join together in any meaningful way. The solution to this was to open their fellowship to all trades, so that any craftsman with an odd assortment of skills could join, and the Order of Odd Fellows (subsequently rendered 'Oddfellows') was set up.

It's not known exactly when the order was set up as monarchs, governments and local authorities were fearful of the working classes organizing themselves for their mutual benefit, so societies preferred secrecy and no official records were ever kept. However, Geoffrey Chaucer does describe a group of guildsmen belonging to a single guild of multiple trades in the prologue to *The Canterbury Tales*, published around the time of the writer's death in 1400.

Throughout the fifteenth and sixteenth centuries, the Oddfellows continued to grow in number and in wealth, leading to an influence that began to be feared by the nobility, who started to regard them as a genuine threat. Although their primary intention was to protect each other against oppression and injustice, the Oddfellows also featured prominently throughout the Catholic Church and when Henry VIII broke with Rome and began the Dissolution of the Monasteries, he also ordered, in 1545, that the property and wealth of the guilds were to be confiscated. The guilds began to unravel but the Oddfellows, who did not rely on a particular trade for their membership, survived the royal oppression and, like the Freemasons (see THE GOAT AND COMPASS), expanded throughout the country, holding their secret meetings in a series of lodges they had established in many major towns. Today any pub or hotel called the **Oddfellows** or the Oddfellows' Arms is likely to have been the venue of their meetings all those years ago.

The Oddfellows also survived the Statute of Apprentices,

passed by Elizabeth I in 1563, that removed the responsibility for regulating apprenticeships from guilds, thus reducing their influence even further, but still the Oddfellows survived and continued to grow, mainly by focusing their efforts on charity and religion. Then, late in the eighteenth century, with the French Revolution in full flow and heads beginning to roll, the government passed a series of laws making membership of guilds such as the Oddfellows a criminal offence, such was its concern about a French-style uprising of the working man. This was the point at which the Oddfellows began destroying all documents and records of members and introduced a system of secret codes by which members would recognize each other. An unusual handshake or a whispered codeword were the signs, and membership became restricted to personal friends and the families of existing members, ensuring government agents could not infiltrate their ranks.

It was around this time, with the onset of the Industrial Revolution, that the modern trade-union movement began to surface, incorporating virtually every principle of the Oddfellows during its own development. During the middle of the nineteenth century, the issue of secret societies again came to the government's attention thanks to a letter from a landowner complaining to the prime minister, Lord Melbourne, that his workers were members of an illegal secret union. Melbourne acted swiftly and ordered the arrest of six men, who were subsequently tried and convicted of swearing a secret oath as members of the Friendly Society of Agricultural Labourers. The men, who famously became known as the Tolpuddle Martyrs, were sentenced to transportation to Australia for a period of seven years, their fate provoking outrage among the British public. Let's be honest, it was barbaric. After all, who would want to spend seven years in Australia if hanging was still an option.

But it was during the twentieth century that the influence of Oddfellow principles and administration upon the lives of the British people really came into its own. By 1911 the Oddfellows incorporated so many ordinary members of the public that prime minister Herbert Asquith used the the society's actuarial tables to calculate contributions and payments when introducing the National Insurance Act, and after the Second World War many Oddfellows administrators were employed to run the new welfare state and National Health Service. To this day, Oddfellows are active throughout Britain as one of the largest friendly and yet secret societies in the world. Well, secret until I just told you all about them, that is.

The Old Dog and Duck
HUNTING, SHOOTING AND . . . LISTENING

There was a time, centuries ago, and well before the advent of the shotgun, when duck hunting was a wildly popular pursuit. In villages all over the land, duck hunting, a favourite pastime of King Charles II, consisted of catching a duck, clipping its wings so it could not fly away, throwing it into the village pond and sending the dogs in after it. Ducks diving under water for safety with dogs splashing around trying to bite them in half provided endless hours of fun for the king and his court although, fortunately for the ducks, later kings had rather kinder hobbies.

Although pubs called the **Dog and Duck** (old or

otherwise) were primarily located in small villages in the countryside, the popularity of the name has caused them to spread to more urban communities and across the world, as far afield as Texas in America and Adelaide in Australia. Duck hunting is no longer carried out in its traditional form, of course, as dogs are no longer used to actually hunt and kill, but just to retrieve the birds for the hunter. At least that's what they claim down at the new Duck and Shotgun.

Dogs, the Englishman's best friend, have long been associated with pubs, giving rise to a host of 'dog'-related names. The **Dog and Bear**, for instance, harks back to the time when bear baiting was popular. The poor animal would be chained to a stake while people set their dogs on it. Bets would then be placed as to how many dogs a bear would kill with its giant paws, or on how many dogs it would take to kill the beast. Like cockfighting (see THE COCK), the 'sport' was outlawed in 1835. Then there is the **Dog and Dart**, referring to how game would at one time be shot by arrows instead of guns, dogs being used to bring back the slaughtered animals or, for a larger creature like a deer, help bring it down. No doubt I could track down a tale of a dog who played darts (these days probably captured in a video on YouTube), but it wouldn't be true.

Other variations include the **Black Dog, Red Dog, Spotted Dog**, the **Dog and Hedgehog** and even the **Dog and Muff** (a joking reference to how elegant ladies, hundreds of years before Paris Hilton, used to carry their tiny pets around). According to local legend, the **Dog and Pot** at Stoke Poges in Buckinghamshire acquired its name because the landlord's lazy wife allowed the pub dog to lick the pots clean and then dry them with his tail – which sounds like a pretty tall (or shaggy dog) tale to me. And then there is the **Dog and Trumpet**: no trumpet-playing dog, this, but a trumpet-listening one, you might say. Pubs bearing this name are relatively recent, going back to 1973, when the HMV record company celebrated its seventy-fifth anniversary. Formed as the Gramophone Company in 1898, it traded under that name until 1909 when it first used the iconic picture of a fox terrier seated next to a gramophone listening to its owner talking to it through the horn (trumpet). The picture, and from that point the company, was entitled His Master's Voice (HMV). The original painting now hangs in the boardroom of EMI records.

The Pickled Parson

THE TRUE TALE OF A RECTOR WHO TURNED TO DRINK –
AFTER HIS DEATH

Now for a story that has never inspired a pub name, but if you are looking for something to call your pub or hotel, you can have this one on me. The rector of Sedgefield, in Country Durham, the Reverend John Garnage, died in December 1747, a week before the tithes were due from the local landowners. Tithes, a tax of one-tenth of the value of the crop produced by a landowner or farmer, were payable to the parish church. Initially this was a voluntary payment but it became compulsory towards the end of the eighth century, making the Church in general fabulously wealthy.

The untimely death of the reverend would have spelled financial disaster for his wife and family as the tithes for the year would have gone instead direct to the Bishop of

Durham, in which case, as history records in so many similar instances, the parson's widow and children would have probably starved. Instead, the good lady acted quickly and kept news of her husband's death to herself, even going to the lengths of preserving his body in brandy until after the 20th of the month when all tithes had been paid. She then dried out the pickled parson and called in the local doctor, who, apparently unaware of her deception but knowing that her husband had liked a drink (or sixteen, judging by the smell), pronounced him dead, dating the death certificate to after 20 December. Legend has it, however, that the reverend, none too pleased at his wife delaying his assent to heaven, returned to haunt the parsonage and disturb the neighbourhood, which he did every evening for over fifty years until a devastating fire finally smoked out his vengeful spirit and he was never heard from again.

Sedgefield was also the parliamentary seat of a certain Tony Blair throughout his political career, including his spell as prime minister of Great Britain. The Pickled Parson or the Pickled Prime Minister. You can take your pick; it's only a matter of time.

The Pig and Whistle

CELEBRATORY FARE OR SOMEWHERE TO DROWN YOUR TROUBLES?

There are three theories behind the pub name the Pig and Whistle: none of them explain the pennywhistle-playing pig pictured on most inn signs. One story has it that in days gone by innkeepers would insist their young employees whistled continuously while down in the cellar, to prove they were not drinking the stock. A 'pig' was a common name for an earthenware pot used to store ale. So the 'pig and whistle' could be an everyday picture of fifteenth-century pub life . . .

Others have pointed out that it is more likely to have something to do with celebration and good times. Hence the 'pig' might be the actual animal, nicely fattened, while the 'whistle' could be a corruption of the old English word 'wassail', a celebratory drink used to toast someone's health. A cup of the spiced ale was passed around at Christmas and New Year in a wassail bowl, as described in 1801 by Joseph Strutt in his *Sports and Pastimes of the People of England*: 'A Wassail Bowl is a bowl of spiced ale formerly carried around by young women on New Year's Eve who went from door to door in their several parishes singing a few couplets of homely verses composed for the purpose and presented the liquor to the inhabitants of the house expecting a small gratuity in return.' I'm not convinced drunken girls and wassail bowls are necessarily the origin of the Pig and Whistle, although I can see why some might think that.

In my view the name is far more likely to be connected with the old English expression 'to go to pigs and whistles', in use around the 1680s and meaning 'to go to rack and ruin'. You can see how 'Pig and Whistle' could easily have become a nickname for a tavern where customers went to drown their troubles, going to rack and ruin if they weren't there already. It's got a similar ring to the popular tavern name THE WORLD'S END – the place to go when the whole world has gone to pot (or pig). There's also the phrase 'to wet your whistle', meaning 'to have a drink', so there could be a connection there, too.

The Prince Blucher

THE TURNCOAT WHO STOPPED NAPOLEON OR HOW BRANDY
WAS USED TO ACHIEVE A FAMOUS VICTORY

There are many Prince Blucher pubs around England, the
most famous being in Twickenham near London, while
others can be found in the north and as far south as Cornwall.

Gebhard Leberecht von Blücher, later Fürst (Prince) of
Wahlstatt (1742–1819), was born in Rostock, a port on
the Baltic Sea and the largest city in the German state of
Mecklenburg, where his family had been prominent landowners since the thirteenth century. At just fourteen years
of age, Blücher joined the Swedish army as a hussar (cavalry soldier – see also THE BRIGADIER GERARD). At the
time, Sweden was at war with Prussia, a major European

power and leading state of the German Empire ruled over by Frederick the Great, in a conflict that became known as the Seven Years' War (see THE MARQUIS OF GRANBY).

During the Pomeranian campaign in 1760, the eighteen-year-old was captured by the Prussian army who were so impressed with his fighting spirit that the colonel in charge invited Blücher to join their ranks as a cavalry officer, and he thus served with distinction for the remaining three years of the war on the opposite side from which he had started. In peacetime, however, his boorish behaviour and ill-discipline – included drinking, petty violence and the abuse of prisoners, such as the staging, in one instance, of a mock execution – meant he was passed over for promotion. Blücher responded to this by sending an insolent letter of resignation in 1773 to Frederick the Great, his commander-in-chief. Unmoved, Frederick, later regarded by Napoleon as the greatest tactical soldier of all time, casually replied: 'Blücher can go to hell.'

Blücher took his commander at his word and, although he didn't literally go to hell, he became a farmer in northern Germany instead, which some might say is close enough. For fifteen long years he farmed the land and adapted to his new peaceful way of life, finding the time to marry and father seven children. Then, on Frederick's death in 1786, the former soldier was invited back and reinstated as major of his old regiment, the Red Hussars. For the next fourteen years Blücher once again fought with distinction and in 1801 was promoted to lieutenant general in recognition of his services.

But it was during the Napoleonic Wars – beginning in 1803 when the eponymous Frenchman started annoying all his European neighbours by invading their lands – that Blücher found worldwide fame and even heroic status. The doughty lieutenant general led the Prussian army on many campaigns against the French, but a crushing defeat for his army and personal humiliation at Ratekau in northern Germany in November 1806 led to a crusade for revenge Napoleon Bonaparte would later live to regret.

After being released in a high-level prisoner exchange, Blücher was promoted to general in charge of the Prussian cavalry and soon had nearly 100,000 men under his command. On 16 October 1813, Blücher (now promoted to field marshal) and his army defeated the French at Möckern, pursuing them all the way back to the French capital throughout the winter of 1813–14. Blücher's actions directly encouraged other European commanders to carry the war into France itself, while his troops won several significant victories, including the vital battle at Laon on 10 March that effectively broke Napoleon's army apart. Still unsatisfied, Blücher pressed on, intending to take revenge on the people of Paris and threatening to sack the city, which he probably would have done had the British not persuaded him otherwise.

On 13 June 1814, Blücher was made a prince in recognition of his achievements and received a welcome fit for a hero everywhere he travelled, especially in Britain. When Napoleon went into exile on the island of Elba, Blücher returned to his farm, but he was re-called to active service within a matter of months.

Napoleon, using his time well, had cunningly planned his revenge. His newly gathered French army shattered Blücher's regiment at Ligny on 16 June 1815, in the course of which the old field marshal was seriously wounded. Lying trapped under his dead horse for several hours, he was repeatedly ridden over by cavalry.

As Napoleon's confident new army turned towards Waterloo and an engagement with the British under the command of the Duke of Wellington (see THE IRON DUKE), Blücher refused to consider the idea of withdrawing his depleted troops. Instead he bathed his wounds with brandy, drank the rest of it and, driven by his now blazing hatred of the French, led his men in pursuit of Napoleon, finally arriving at Waterloo as the battle had already started and the outcome hung in the balance. But Blücher's intervention proved decisive and between them the Prussian prince and the British duke devastated Bonaparte's army in a crushing defeat.

After the battle, Blücher is believed to have turned to Wellington and commented, in what was probably the understatement of the century, 'My dear comrade, what an affair.'

Wellington returned to England a national hero, while Blücher retired to Poland, where he died peacefully four years later, in 1819. To this day, Germans use the expression *ran wie Blücher* ('on it like Blücher') to describe approaching a task with aggressive determination. Statues in his honour have been erected in many German towns and, nearly two hundred years after his death, pubs in Britain still bear the name of the war hero, whose courage and tenacity turned the Battle of Waterloo in Britain's favour, putting an end, once and for all, to the Napoleonic threat.

The Prospect of Whitby
(Wapping, London)

THE PLACE TO GO FOR A RINGSIDE VIEW OF EXECUTION
DOCK

Situated on the banks of the Thames at Wapping, the
Prospect is one of London's most famous pubs. It also
claims to be one of its oldest: a tavern has served ale on
the site since 1520. During the seventeenth century the
pub had a reputation as a den of thieves and smugglers
and became known as the Devil's Tavern. During the
same century the famous diarist Samuel Pepys (1633–
1703) became a regular customer when he was attending
naval business in Wapping. The notorious 'Hanging'
Judge Jeffreys (1645–89) – who earned his harsh reputation during the trials following the Monmouth Rebellion
of 1685 – was also a regular and would watch the hang-
ings at nearby Execution Dock (see also THE CAPTAIN
KIDD) from the pub balcony. Common criminals were
tied to posts here and left to drown as the tide came in.
During the late eighteenth or early nineteenth century a
fire destroyed the Devil's Tavern. Once the pub had been
rebuilt, the landlord clearly thought its image could do
with a boost. Hence it was renamed after a three-masted
collier from the north-east that regularly moored alongside, the *Prospect of Whitby*.

The Quiet Woman
HOW HOLDING YOUR TONGUE CAN HELP YOU KEEP YOUR HEAD

The Quiet Woman is one name I simply had to investigate, having never encountered one myself. (I mean the pub, of course.) The Quiet Woman in East Sterndale, near Buxton in Derbyshire is over four hundred years old, owned by the same family for over three hundred. The pub sign bears the picture of a headless woman with the legend: 'Soft words turneth away wrath.' The story goes that there was once an innkeeper's wife in Earl Sterndale who was so talkative that her head was cut off in a final attempt to silence her. Either more than one chatty woman met a similar grisly fate or the variations on the theme – including the **Good Woman** and the **Headless Woman** – all refer to the same legend, reinforced by the rhyme: 'Here is a woman who has lost her head / She is all quiet now – you see she is dead.'

The Quiet Woman in Leek, Staffordshire, has a similar sign – a woman carrying her head in one hand and a candelabrum in the other. The story goes that she was a treacherous barmaid who was punished for spreading her customers' secrets. Meanwhile, in Wareham Forest, Dorset, the **Silent Woman Inn** is said to have been a den of smugglers who discovered the landlady had been gossiping about their activities in the local market place. The smugglers silenced her by cutting out her tongue, thereby creating the 'unique phenomenon' of the silent woman.

So, overall, it would appear these pub names have all evolved from the perceived belief that women, in general, talk too much. Pubs are places where men have traditionally sought refuge from the intrusive chatter of their wives (see also THE NAG'S HEAD). To call your pub the Quiet Woman and to hang a picture of a headless woman outside nails your misogynistic colours firmly to the mast: women are not welcome here. It certainly goes to show that humour has got subtler over the centuries. Come back, Bernard Manning – all is forgiven.

The Ram Jam
A DRINK, A CON-TRICK OR THE MOST CROWDED PUB IN TOWN?

The Ram Jam is a common enough name for a pub, club or hotel, but explanations of its origin vary. One tells the tale of an innkeeper who returned from India with the recipe for a new drink that became instantly popular with his regulars, but as it was so easy to make he kept the recipe secret, insisting only his Indian manservant, Ram Jam, knew what it was. He died with the secret intact and locals renamed the pub in honour of their favourite, if no longer available, tipple.

Another, rather more anecdotal theory, from the Ram Jam Inn at Oakham in Leicestershire, apparently accounts for how the pub acquired its unusual name. Many years ago a traveller once claimed he could show the innkeeper's wife how to draw both mild ale and bitter from the same barrel. When she asked for proof, the traveller drilled a hole in one side of the barrel and asked her to ram her thumb into it to prevent the ale from leaking out. Then he made a hole on the other side and insisted she jam her thumb into that while he went to find some spiles (wooden pegs used to control the flow of carbon dioxide from a barrel of beer). But instead, and I think we all saw this one coming, he skipped town without paying his bill, leaving the red-faced wife over the barrel where her husband later found her. The problem with this 'official' version is that I have heard this story told several times as an urban legend, and the pub in question is not always called the Ram Jam.

The final theory is rather duller, if somewhat more likely. The expression 'ram jam' was already well known by the early 1800s and understood to mean either a public place full of people or a mouth full of food. More recently the name Ram Jam has acquired a musical connotation. During the 1960s the Ram Jam Club in Brixton became famous for its mixture of ska, reggae and soul music that became popular with the original mods. Ram Jam was also the name of an American rock band that had a world-wide hit in 1977 with a song called 'Black Betty'.

The Red Lion
A WAR WAGED THROUGH PUB NAMES

One of the most popular pub names in Britain, the Red Lion has an interesting history. One theory claims the reason there are so many Red Lions was due to James VI of Scotland becoming James I of England and Ireland, on 24 March 1603 (see also THE BRITANNIA). The red lion was the Scottish king's personal crest and a prominent part of his coat of arms and it is recorded that he ordered the emblem to be displayed at all public places to remind his English subjects that the Scots now held power in the south. Many innkeepers throughout England felt it wise to follow the new rules in case the king and his army happened to ride by one day. While it is certainly due to James I that the red lion became part of the coat of arms of the British monarchy, the idea that this is the source of all those pub and hotel names is, however, doubtful.

The Red Lion was in fact a popular choice of name long before 1603. England's first permanent theatre, built in Mile End in 1567, was called the Red Lion and that was a full thirty-six years before James turned up in England claiming the throne. As many other Red Lions predate his reign, we need to look elsewhere for the origin of the name – to an earlier royal family, in fact, and another coat of arms.

In the fourteenth century John of Gaunt (1340–99) was the most powerful man in England. The third son of King Edward III, he was twenty-seven when his ten-year-old nephew, son of his brother the Black Prince, inherited the English crown as Richard II. Gaunt exercised great influence in the early days of Richard's reign, and not always positively. It was his unwise decisions about various taxes that brought on the Peasants' Revolt in 1381 (see JACK STRAW'S CASTLE), as the rebels recognized when they ransacked Gaunt's Savoy Palace in London (now the site of today's Savoy Hotel).

In 1386 John of Gaunt left England to claim the throne of Castile (he had married Infanta Constance of Castile fifteen years before), whose coat of arms, consisting of a Spanish castle and a red lion, he had incorporated into his own crest. During his absence things soon fell apart, however, and England teetered on the brink of civil war as a result of misrule by the young king. It is thought that many places, including taverns and inns, then began displaying John of Gaunt's coat of arms in order to show their preference for Edward III's surviving son. Highly sensitive to this public vote of no confidence, Richard II responded by ruling that every publican and landlord close to London must display his own crest, THE WHITE HART, instead. Not so different from today, when you think about it, with signs for political candidates popping up everywhere, just before an election, instead of royal coats of arms.

Rather than take advantage of the situation and seize the crown for himself, Gaunt returned to England to support his nephew and help restore stability. Recognized as the real power behind the throne, he enjoyed the wealth and riches of rule and was astute enough to avoid making serious enemies along the way. Even so, he was unable to prevent his ambitious son Henry Bolingbroke being sent into exile by the king in 1398. A year later, Gaunt passed away, dying peacefully in his bed at Leicester Castle. Rather unusually for the time, it was from natural causes. With that his family crest, red lion included, passed over to Henry, while Richard claimed all his lands for the crown.

Henry invaded England in June 1399 with a small force that quickly grew in numbers. Claiming initially that his goal was only to reclaim his patrimony, it soon became clear that he had his eyes firmly fixed on the throne itself. Meeting little resistance, partly thanks to the reputation of his father and partly due to the king's unpopularity, Bolingbroke was able to demonstrate he had enough strength and support to force Richard to hand over the crown, and he became King Henry IV.

Richard died in captivity early the next year; it is thought he was probably murdered. The White Hart had finally, and very definitely, given way to the Red Lion.

The Rising Sun

BACK FROM THE DEAD EACH MORNING

From the dawn of human history, the sun, so vital for life, has been central to people's belief systems. The Aztecs, for example, believed the sun and the earth had already been destroyed four times and that during the time of the fifth sun the final destruction would occur. To ensure the sun continued to rise each day and the world didn't end in disaster, human sacrifices were made to the sun god, Huitzilopochtli, as a key part of their ritual worship. The victim, usually a captured prisoner, would be placed on

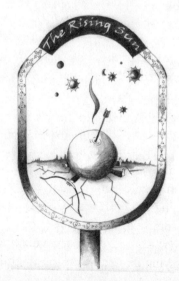

an altar of rounded stone with his back arched and limbs held firm. Then the priest would cut through the abdomen, just below the rib cage, with a flint blade. The heart would be torn out and held, still beating, towards the sky in honour of the sun god.

The sun's return every morning could never be taken for granted, and many cultures evolved myths to explain the cycle of night and day. The ancient Greeks had Helios, riding a chariot across the sky; the Hindu sun god, Surya, also rides a chariot, drawn by seven white horses; the Egyptians had Ra, sailing a barge; while the Chinese saw the sun as a bird slowly flying across the sky. Other myths tell how the sun god dies each night and then comes back to life with the new day.

In 274 the pragmatic Romans (see THE BRITANNIA) created a new sun god, Sol Invictus (the Unconquered Sun), in an attempt to co-opt a whole series of local, heliocentric religions throughout their Eastern provinces. His birthday was celebrated by the Romans on the day after the winter solstice (the shortest day) to signify the rebirth and regrowth of the sun every year. Interestingly, this is when the equally pragmatic Christian Church claims Jesus Christ, too, was born. It couldn't have hurt that many aspects of Christ's story are similar to those of the sun gods of other religions: he sacrificed his life to save the world (the sky was supposed to have turned black as night at his death) and then he was reborn. He was also the Son (sun) of God. And in many churches the image of the rising sun represents Christ's rising from the dead and his promise of eternal life.

Edward III (1312–77), who was extremely keen to emphasize the symbolic nature of the English monarchy (see THE GEORGE AND DRAGON and THE STAR AND GARTER), was said to have decorated his recreation of King Arthur's Round Table with a painting of the rising sun. He was also the first of a number of monarchs who used the sun as one of their royal badges, Edward's emblem being represented as a sunburst, or a golden sun with rays shooting upwards from a bank of white cloud, just like the rising sun. A number of noble families consequently adopted it as part of their coat of arms to enhance their prestige; the many pubs throughout Britain called the Rising Sun are most likely named after them. But it probably doesn't hurt to mention another, bawdier meaning of the name that anyone brought up on the Animals' song 'The House of the Rising Sun' (regarded by many as a euphemism for a brothel) or familiar with John Donne's poem 'The Sun Rising' will recognize . . .

The Robert Peel

MAN OF PRINCIPLES WHO GAVE US THE BOYS IN BLUE

There are many Robert Peels the length and breadth of Britain, and there is a very good reason for that. Robert Peel (1788–1850) enjoyed a long and distinguished political career. He became home secretary in 1822 and again, under the premiership of the Duke of Wellington (see THE IRON DUKE), in 1828, and he was twice elected prime minister, in 1834 and again in 1841. But had it not been for his time as home secretary he might not have been remembered with much affection at all, and certainly we would not be drinking in pubs that bear his name.

In the seventeenth and eighteenth centuries, each

parish had a constable. This system comprised, generally, one unarmed, able-bodied citizen in each parish, who was appointed to serve for a year, unpaid. He would work in cooperation with the local justices in ensuring laws were observed and order maintained. In towns, responsibility for the maintenance of order was conferred on the guilds (see THE ODDFELLOWS' ARMS) and, later, on other specified groups of citizens, and these supplied bodies of paid men, known as the 'watch', for guarding the town gates and patrolling the streets at night (see THE LAMPLIGHTERS). If you had been the victim of a crime, you could hire a thief-taker to track down the perpetrator, but there was no state-run centralized system.

Towards the end of the eighteenth century, with the onset of the Industrial Revolution, great socio-economic changes were afoot, leading to a huge influx of people into the towns. London had always been a hive of criminal activity. But as the city grew ever larger, it became harder to control and the parish constable and 'watch' systems were unable to cope. There had been various private attempts at policing, most notably by Henry Fielding's Bow Street Runners in 1749, but as there were just eight of them, there was only so much that they could do. And it wasn't just crime. London was also a centre for political unrest. The second half of the eighteenth century had seen the city racked by three major uprisings against the government: the Strand Riots (protesting against 'disorderly houses') in 1749; the 1768 Wilkes Riots (caused by attempts to prevent the electorate choosing their own MP); and the Gordon Riots (protesting about Catholics being given equal rights) in 1780, which caused huge destruction and had to be stopped by the army.

The French Revolution then provided a vivid illustration in 1789–99 of what an angry populace could do if their needs and demands continued to be ignored. Britain needed reform and London desperately needed a centralized police force. Unfortunately this went against the English respect for individual liberty, desire for self-regulation and distrust of the state: surveillance of any kind was hotly resented. Parliamentary committees were set up in 1812, 1818 and 1822 to look into the subject of crime and policing. But it was not until 1828 when Sir Robert Peel set up a further committee that progress was finally made, resulting in a bill that led to the setting up of an organized police force in London.

The Metropolitan Police Act was reluctantly passed by Parliament in 1829. To allay the fears of an alarmed and suspicious public, the first policemen had to wear their distinctive uniform even when off duty, so that they could never be accused of concealing their identity; they put an armband on when on duty.

Starting with just 1,000 uniformed men, who were known either as 'Bobbies' or 'Peelers' (after Sir Robert), 'coppers' (they caught or 'copped' villains) or 'crushers' (they crushed liberty), Peel's civilian force were initially highly unpopular: in fact, juries at the inquests of two of the first officers killed on duty, PC Joseph Grantham and PC Robert Culley, returned verdicts of justifiable homicide. Gradually, however, the tide of public opinion turned in the police's favour when they proved very effective at reducing crime in the capital.

And so other police forces were rapidly established throughout Britain and its growing colonies. Since then, Robert Peel has come to be regarded as the father of modern policing while his Peelian Principles define the core values for a successful police force. There are nine of them and although well over a hundred and fifty years old, they are still equally valid today. Here are three of the most resonant:

> The ability of the police force to perform their duties is dependent upon public approval of police actions.

> The test of police efficiency is the absence of crime and disorder, not the visible evidence of police action in dealing with it.

> The police at all times should maintain a relationship with the public that gives reality to the historic tradition that the police are the public and the public are the police.

The Robin Hood
THE PERFECT COMPANION FOR AN EVENING AT THE PUB?

Robin Hood is one of the great English heroes. For generations we have been told about this lovable bandit who famously stole from the rich and gave to the poor and who lived with his Merry Men in Sherwood Forest, near Nottingham. Over the years he has been the subject of songs and ballads, radio and TV programmes, novels, films, paintings and poems. He has been portrayed as a farmer, archer, nobleman, hero, traitor and common thief, but what do we really know about him?

The earliest written reference to Robin appears in William Langland's *Piers Plowman* (c.1360–87). In it,

THE ROBIN HOOD

a character called Sloth admits that while he can't always remember his prayers, he knows all the ballads of popular heroes, especially those of Robin Hood by heart. The allegorical story of an ordinary man's path to enlightenment, *Piers Plowman* is a poem of protest against the contemporary corruption and inadequacy of the Church and state. Rather like a *Private Eye* of its time, it poked a satirical finger at the establishment, and in so doing is believed to have influenced the Peasants' Revolt (see JACK STRAW'S CASTLE). The ballads of Robin Hood, not written down until the fifteenth century, are jollier and lighter than *Piers Plowman* but they also tell the story of one man who manages to trick the rich and powerful and gives their wealth to the people who need it, the poor. Unlike King Arthur, Robin Hood is a hero for ordinary people who constantly gets away with tweaking the nose of the overly privileged, and consequently the ballads became incredibly popular. But just because he was a much needed figure for yesterday's peasants and today's tourist industry, it doesn't mean that he wasn't a real person.

Many people believe that Robin Hood actually existed, living around the end of the twelfth or beginning of the thirteenth century. In Sherwood Forest the tree he supposedly lived in, the Major Oak, has been carbon-dated at 800–1,000 years old, meaning that it would have been old even in Robin's day, which correlates with the legend. The problem is that different ballads tell different stories and a lot of the evidence is doubled up as both Yorkshire and Nottingham claim him as their own. Among the sites associated with his name is Kirklees Priory, in west Yorkshire, which claims to have his tombstone, dated 1247 and apparently fitting with the account of Robin's death in which he is killed by his cousin, the Prioress of Kirklees, when he travels to visit her at the priory. Equally, he could be buried at Loxley, near Stratford-upon-Avon (possibly the Lockersley cited in the ballads as his birthplace?), in which the churchyard has a grave with the name of Robert Fitz Odo (another of Robin's pseudonyms) and dating to the thirteenth century.

So could it be that there was more than one Robin Hood? Or that every tale about outlaws was rounded up under the name of the most popular one? (It's what happened to Dick Turpin in the eighteenth century, when all stories about highwaymen were attributed to him. See THE CROOKED BILLET for more on him.) That would certainly explain some of the known discrepancies in the information that we have. After all, the stories were in the form of ballads and in the constant retelling all kinds of extra details and contemporary touches would have been added to suit the times and changing tastes of their listeners.

It's easy to see why so many pubs are named after him. If Robin Hood was a real man, he would have been a great person to spend a long evening in the pub with. Not to mention the fact that the Merry Men would have made the perfect medieval pub quiz team. I'm thinking about a time when the sport round would have just covered wrestling (**Little John's** favourite subject) and archery, **Friar Tuck** would have tackled food- and drink-related questions, **Alan a Dale** contemporary music and **Maid Marian** etiquette and embroidery. No wonder there are also pubs named after all of them.

The Rose and Crown

EMBLEM OF TWO FEUDING FAMILIES FINALLY UNITED

The rose is by far the most frequently occurring flower when it comes to pub names, and there is a good reason for this. The popular pub sign of a red-and-white rose and a crown is the symbol of the ending of a civil war that, for many years, tore the country apart.

In the fifteenth century there were two English dynasties that used a rose as their emblem: the House of York had a white rose and the House of Lancaster a red one. When Henry Bolingbroke seized the throne in 1399, becoming Henry IV (see THE RED LION), it was the House of Lancaster that took over the throne. He was succeeded by the even more able Henry V (see THE AGINCOURT). Unfortunately, the king that followed, Henry

VI, was not only mentally unstable (something he had inherited from his mad French grandfather, who had believed he was made of glass) but was also just a child when he took over the throne.

As long as Henry had no sons, his ambitious cousin Richard of York was his heir. Seeking to minimize this threat, the king sent Richard into virtual exile in France and then in Ireland. In 1452 Richard returned secretly to England, attempting to rally support in his aim to be officially recognized as Henry's heir, but with his army defeated he was forced to swear an oath of allegiance and abandon his claim to power. Then the following year things looked up for him as the king suffered what appears to have been a complete mental collapse.

York's hour had come, it seemed, and Richard was appointed Protector of the Realm, overruling opposition by Henry's strong-willed French wife, Margaret of Anjou. But the king recovered and it was back to square one for the duke, who gathered another army, meeting Henry at St Albans on 22 May 1455. In the subsequent battle York was lined up against Lancaster, the first in a series of engagements in what became known as the War of the Roses. In this instance it was an emphatic victory for York, the duke taking the king prisoner and appointing himself Constable of England.

In custody, the king became ill again. Richard remained confident the royal couple were out of the action – and, in the case of the king, out of his mind – but he had underestimated the resolve of Margaret, who not only nursed her husband back to mental health but also raised the support of an army, settling it near Coventry, one of the few parts of England where Henry VI was still popular.

This tense political situation overshadowed England for over thirty years, with attack and counter-attack between the two warring families as the War of the Roses dragged on. Even after Richard of York himself was killed at the Battle of Wakefield in December 1460 (an historic event said to have given rise to the mnemonic that enables children to memorize the colours of the rainbow: Richard Of York Gave Battle In Vain – red, orange, yellow, green, blue, indigo and violet), which should have put an end to the dispute, his son Edward, the new Duke of York, simply took over the reins and kept the conflict going.

It was during the period of the War of the Roses that innkeepers would show their allegiance either to the king or to the Duke of York by displaying a red rose or a white one outside their establishments. Some canny landlords would have had both, switching from one to the other as appropriate. But this all came to an end soon after the Battle of Bosworth in 1485, after which the Lancastrian Henry Tudor established himself as King Henry VII, cleverly scotching the competition by immediately marrying Elizabeth of York. With the Houses of York and Lancaster finally united, their family symbols were also merged to form the famous red-and-white Tudor rose. Encouraged to show loyalty to both royal houses, innkeepers now displayed the bicoloured rose and the royal crown.

The Royal Oak

THE TREE THAT GAVE REFUGE TO A STUART KING ON THE RUN

On 30 January 1649, King Charles I of England and Scotland, wearing two shirts to avoid any shivering that

might be mistaken for fear, climbed on to the scaffold outside the Banqueting House in London's Whitehall and was beheaded (see THE KING'S HEAD). This event was intended to mark the end of the English Civil War and the victory of Oliver Cromwell's New Model Army over the English monarchy.

But as the saying goes, 'The king is dead! Long live the king!' and his eighteen-year-old son, Charles, was soon proclaimed King of Scotland, an entirely separate kingdom at the time. Before long, the boy king was leading an army south to drive out Cromwell. By the spring of 1651, his force of 14,000 well-armed men had crossed the border into England.

However, Cromwell, the great military strategist, had already sent Parliamentarian forces north to disarm suspected Royalist sympathizers by confiscating weapons and horses from the country estates and securing them for his own use in secret locations. As a result, Charles failed to raise any meaningful support on his journey south, and when his army of just over 16,000 men reached Worcester, he was met by a well-prepared and determined force of nearly 30,000 battle-hardened Parliamentarian troops. Early on the morning of 3 September 1651, Cromwell ordered his field commanders to attack Royalist positions around the town and the Battle of Worcester was over within a few short hours. By mid afternoon Charles's forces were on the run.

His advisers agreed that the king would be safer and draw less attention in a smaller group and one of his companions, Charles Giffard, took him to the White Ladies Priory (where, legend has it, Guinevere retired after the death of King Arthur) and then to Boscobel House on the Shropshire and Staffordshire border in the early hours of 4 September. With Cromwell's men hard on their heels, Giffard knew they had to move fast. A reward of £1,000, a vast sum of money in 1651, had already been offered for his capture: anybody found to be hiding him was certain to be executed. In an attempt to disguise the king to help prevent his capture, Charles's distinctive thick, black curly hair was cut short and he was dressed as a simple woodsman.

Tipped off that Cromwell's forces were closing in, Giffard had nowhere else to go and he was desperate to hide the king. Charles himself later recalled the story for Samuel Pepys:

> [Giffard] told me that it would be very dangerous to either stay in the house or go into the wood . . . that he knew but one way how to pass the next day, and that was to get up into the great oak, in a pretty plain place where we might

see round about us, for the enemy would certainly search at the wood for people that had made their escape. Of which proposition I approving, we went and carried with us some victuals [provisions] for the whole day, viz. bread, cheese, small beer, and nothing else, and got up into a great oak that had been lopped three or four years before, and being grown out again very bushy and thick, could not be seen through, and here we stayed all day . . . While we were in this tree we saw soldiers going up and down in the thicket of the wood, searching for persons escaped, we seeing them, now and then, peeping out of the wood.

It took another six weeks of disguises and adventures before the young king was finally smuggled to safety in France. Charles then stayed in exile until 1660 when he finally returned to London on his thirtieth birthday, 29 May. In 1664 this day was made, by Act of Parliament, a national holiday to mark the restoration and officially called 'Oak Apple Day' in honour of the oak tree at Boscobel that had successfully concealed the king and protected him, years earlier, from certain death.

For nearly two hundred years, Oak Apple Day was celebrated all over the land. It was a hugely popular festival. Everyone, high and low, male and female, adult and child, would wear a spray of oak leaves in their lapel or hat: traditionally any child not wearing such an emblem was attacked unmercifully by their schoolfellows and could be pinched, stung with nettles or pelted with rotten eggs. And many taverns and inns were named the Royal Oak to demonstrate their loyalty and support for the monarchy.

By the early 1700s the original oak tree had been all but destroyed by souvenir hunters although, from a single acorn, another fine oak tree has grown alongside the site of the original, called the 'Son of Royal Oak'. In 2001 Prince Charles, the future King Charles III, planted a sapling alongside this tree after it was severely damaged in a storm. Grown from one of the tree's acorns, this makes it 'Grandson of Royal Oak'.

To this day, there are thought to be over six hundred pubs and hotels bearing the name the Royal Oak, making it one of the most popular pub names in Britain. In many cases the traditional pub sign depicts a great oak tree and, if you look hard enough, you may just be able to make out the young king peeping through the branches somewhere near the top.

The Sandboys

THE YOUNG WORKERS WHO FOUND HAPPINESS AT THE BOTTOM OF A BOTTLE

In *The Old Curiosity Shop* (1841) Dickens describes an inn called the Jolly Sandboys, which has a sign outside depicting three drunken lads, or, as he puts it: 'increasing their jollity with as many jugs of ale'. A moment of creative licence from the great man? Not if you look back a few years and find Dickens is known to have spent some time in Bristol, a place he also refers to in his 1836 novel *The Pickwick Papers*.

In those days the town's landlords would spread sand on the floor of their inns and pubs to soak up any spillages, much in the way that sawdust would have been used in other establishments. The Redcliffe Caves in Bristol were known for the fine sand they contained, which was

chiefly used for making glass bottles. The sand was also used for ship's ballast and for sprinkling on floors. Hence innkeepers would send young lads off into the caves to provide them with a regular supply. Being a sandboy was extremely thirsty work and the youngsters were famous for their bottomless capacity for beer. They were partly paid in ale and consequently were usually half cut – hence Dickens's invention 'the jolly sandboy' and the related phrase 'happy as a sandboy'. Many pubs around Bristol used sandboys and some adopted the term as a name.

The Saracen's Head
GRISLY MEMENTO FROM THE CRUSADES?

The reason there are so many Saracen's Heads in Britain can be traced back to the Crusades, the series of military campaigns that took place in the Middle East between 1095 and 1291, pitting Christians against Muslims. It all began in March 1095 when the Pope (in this case Pope Urban II) called upon all good Christian nations to wage a holy war to recapture Jerusalem and the Holy Land from Muslim rule and to prevent the expansion of the Seljuk Turks into Anatolia (essentially modern Turkey). The Seljuk Turks are better known today as Sunni Muslims, the largest denomination of Islam.

The Crusaders referred to their adversaries as 'Saracens', derived from the Arabic word 'easterners' but seemingly interpreted by them as 'people I want to kill'. Indeed, in those days, the warring knights of England managed to slaughter their foes in quite impressive numbers. Legend has it that, on returning to their estates and castles, some brought with them the heads of their Saracen victims as souvenirs. As the Crusades progressed over the decades, many noble families were granted the privilege of using a Saracen's head as part of their family coat of arms, leading to the long association retained to this day. And hopefully one that will continue, although a Saracen's Head pub in Birmingham was recently forced to change its name, for fear of offending Muslims, which will no doubt lead to a campaign for name changes everywhere on grounds of political correctness. Not a crusade I'll be joining, that's for sure.

In more recent times, King Charles I spent his last night as a free man at the **King's Arms** in Southwell, Nottinghamshire, before surrendering to the Scots, who promptly handed him over to Cromwell. After the king's execution in 1649 (see THE KING'S HEAD), the inn changed its name to the Saracen's Head to show allegiance to Oliver Cromwell's New Model Army (maybe in mocking reference to Charles's dark complexion) and it has kept the name ever since.

The Seven Sisters
THE SEVEN DAUGHTERS OF ATLAS WHO WERE TRANSFORMED INTO STARS

There are Seven Sisters throughout the world, the name applied both to natural formations – mountains, caves and waterfalls – and manmade ones: skyscrapers, churches and, of course, pubs. Some historians have suggested the chalk cliffs at Seaford on the south coast of England provide the origin of the pub name. But this is hard to justify, especially as I counted eight of them when I was last there. Or perhaps the area of the same name to the north of Tottenham in London may hold the key. Originally called after the seven famous elm trees thought to have been over five hundred years old when they were removed in 1840, they were symbolically replaced in 1885 by the seven Hibbert sisters. In 1955 the trees were again replanted, this time by the seven Basten sisters of north London.

But the real origin of the Seven Sisters can be traced much further back, to a cluster of seven stars called the Pleiades, used by mariners long ago to navigate their way at night. It is this famous and easily visible cluster of stars, part of the Taurus constellation, that has provided the inspiration for the eponymous pub sign, not to mention all those natural and manmade formations.

The Pleiades has played a part in many cultures throughout the world, each with a different story to tell about how the constellation came into being. In Australia the indigenous peoples believe the seven sisters were being chased by a man called Jilbi Tjakamarra and were transformed into stars to escape him, but then Jilbi transformed himself into the Morning Star and continues to chase them across the sky. In China the Pleiades are known as the Hairy Head of the White Tiger in the West, a mythological guardian of the skies. A Cheyenne legend called 'The Girl Who Married a Dog' claims the seven stars were the seven puppies a chief's daughter gave birth to after being visited by a dog in human form. In parts of Europe the seven stars are believed to have been seven maidens who were taken to the heavens to dance for the gods, while the Vikings maintained they were the seven hens of Freya, the goddess of love.

In Greek mythology the original seven sisters were the seven daughters of Atlas, the Titan who supported the planet upon his broad shoulders, but then if you had been paying attention during Classics lessons at school, you'd already know that. Atlas's daughters, Maia, Electra, Taygete, Alcyone, Celaeno, Sterope and Merope, were beautiful nymphs, six of whom engaged in love affairs with the Olympian gods, including Zeus and Poseidon. These represent the six stars of the Pleiades that shine brightly. One of the stars, however, much dimmer than the rest, represents Merope, who is being shamed for eternity for having an affair with, and becoming pregnant by, a mere mortal, like you and me. So the next time you are drinking in the Seven Sisters, or the **Seven Stars,** you will know which one to look out for.

The Spion Kop
THE HEROIC DEFEAT COMMEMORATED BY PUBS AND FOOTBALL STANDS

The Spion Kop, a rather unusual name for a pub, comes from a notorious battle in the Second Boer War (1899–1902). During the battle, Spion Kop – which, literally translated, means 'the big hill to spy from' (a small hill is a *koppie*) – was occupied by the Boers (white South Africans). On 23 January 1900, a very foggy night, the Boer lookouts were surprised by around fifteen British soldiers. The British drove the Boers from the Kop and, after being joined by a further 1,000 men, they then dug in their own defensive positions.

But as dawn broke and the fog cleared, the British were horrified to realize they were actually holding only a lower peak and the Boers were on higher ground, surrounding three sides of their position. When a Pretoria Commando unit scaled the rocky kop, they were completely surrounded, at which the Boers seized the opportunity and began to attack.

With their backs against the wall, the British fought valiantly, and despite heavy odds the Boers were forced back on several occasions although casualties were high on both sides. A young Winston Churchill who was in South Africa as a war correspondent, and who had recently escaped from Boer captivity, acted as a courier between the front line and British army headquarters. He noted at the time: 'Corpses lay here and there. Many of the wounds were of a horrible nature as splinters and fragments from the shells had torn and mutilated them.

The shallow trenches were choked with the dead and wounded.' As darkness fell, the British launched a ferocious attack, gaining the higher ground, and the guns fell silent for the night.

Early the next morning the British commanders, unaware that the Boers had withdrawn during the early hours, ordered their own soldiers off the kop after hearing they were running low on ammunition and had no water. The retreating Boers were thus amazed to find the kop occupied by two of their burghers (civilians), waving down from the peak at them, with no British in sight except the dead and soon to be dead. The result was a rare but significant victory for the Boers: over 1,300 British were either wounded or captured; 243 were dead and many remain buried on the kop. But although the British had retreated, the Boers were too weak to take advantage of their victory and by the end of the year the British returned in numbers to crush the Boer uprising.

An ignominious British defeat seems an unusual choice of name for a pub, but it's the courage of the soldiers, let down by the poor decisions of their commanders, that is being celebrated. The battle has even lent its name to an English village, near Mansfield in Nottinghamshire. And its name has provided inspiration in the sporting world, too. In 1904, four years after the event, a journalist likened the silhouette of the football fans standing on a newly raised bank of earth at the Woolwich Arsenal football ground to soldiers standing atop Spion Kop. Two years later, another journalist, Ernest Edwards, commented on the newly built open-air embankment at Liverpool's famous Anfield Stadium: 'This huge wall of earth has been termed "Spion Kop", and no doubt this apt name will always be used in future in referring to this spot.' Shortened to the 'Kop', it's now one of the most recognized venues in the world of football.

The Spofforth
(Edge Hill, Liverpool)

THE DEMON BOWLER WHOSE VICTORY OVER ENGLAND
INSPIRED THE ASHES

Also in Liverpool is a pub simply known as the Spofforth, taking its name from the Australian cricketer Fred Spofforth (1853–1926). Feared by batsmen around the world as the 'Demon Bowler', and the first man ever to achieve a hat-trick in test match cricket (three wickets taken by a bowler in three consecutive balls), Spofforth was, according to another cricketing legend, W. G. Grace, the 'most difficult bowler I have ever played against'.

It was Fred Spofforth's highly effective technique of 'eye-balling' a batsman after each delivery, used to devastating effect during the test match in 1882, that gave birth to the famous Ashes series. With England needing only eighty-five runs from their second innings for victory, Spofforth rallied his team and famously shouted: 'Boys, this thing can be done.' And the Australians narrowly won by seven runs, Spofforth taking a decisive fourteen wickets in the process. The next morning the *Sporting Times* wrote a famously satirical obituary for English cricket, declaring: 'The body will be cremated and the ashes taken to Australia.' The following year journalists wrote of the English tour of Australia as 'the quest to bring back the ashes', and so the legend was born, largely thanks to Fred Spofforth.

Sports fans were rather more forgiving in the nineteenth century and when he moved to England in 1888, Spofforth was welcomed with open arms, so much so that he rapidly got married to an English girl. He then played for various English teams, including Derbyshire and the MCC (see LORD'S TAVERN), before turning to business, becoming managing director of the Star Tea Company. Proving himself to be as capable in business as he was talented on the cricket field, Spofforth steered the company to great success. At his death in 1926, he left a fortune of £165,000, a princely sum in those days. The combination of the two quintessential English loves (cricket and tea) had clearly civilized the Demon Bowler.

The Spread Eagle

PROUD SYMBOL OF A NATION OR A CRUEL FORM OF PUNISHMENT?

While the lion has long been regarded the king of the beasts, the eagle is the queen of the skies and, for that reason, the bird most favoured as a heraldic symbol. Implying courage, strength and immortality, the eagle was considered by the ancient Greeks to be Zeus's messenger; the Romans also associated it with their king of the gods, Jupiter, and made it the symbol of their empire. To identify themselves to the enemy, Roman legions would display three or four standards (see THE STANDARD), the most important of these being the legionary eagle, made of fine silver and carried by a standard bearer wearing a lionskin headdress. This eagle had its wings proudly spread in domination.

An image of an eagle with wings and talons outstretched has been connected with dynasties stretching across the world, from England to Germany, Poland, Romania, Serbia and Austria. In America the bald eagle, the national bird of the United States, famously appears, wings and talons outspread, on the great seal of office, designed by Charles Thomson in June 1782. (Interestingly, this was the source of the American expression 'spread-eaglism', describing extreme patriotism in the form of aggressive foreign policy.) Any of these could have inspired the image used on pub signs. Indeed, displaying a royal or aristocratic crest has long been how landlords and hotel owners have shown their loyalty to the monarchy or local ruling family. While Napoleon Bonaparte also used the spread eagle on his own crest, a symbol retained by the House of Bonaparte to this day, I doubt this has inspired any English pub signs, unless the bird also had Wellington's boot aimed at its backside (see THE IRON DUKE).

But the pub name could also have been referring to something rather more ghoulish. During the seventeenth and eighteenth centuries, the Royal Navy's punishments for disobedience, absenteeism and even relatively minor offences were unimaginably brutal. It was common for a crew member to be tied to a mast or over a cannon with his arms and legs outstretched in a position known as the 'spread eagle', after which he would be subjected to however many lashes of a cat o' nine tails the captain deemed necessary. A 'cat' consisted of nine lengths of thin-knotted rope bound at one end into a handle, while the flogging was usually carried out by one of the victim's shipmates in full view of the rest of the crew. But as it was also likely that the shipmate would himself be a victim of the cat o' nine tails at some stage on a voyage, he would tend to be lenient with his victim, applying only light stokes and merely 'scratching' the fellow's back. He himself would then receive equally lenient treatment by another shipmate if he was ever on the receiving end, which led to the expression 'You scratch my back and I'll scratch yours'.

The Standard
HOW THE THREE LIONS OF ENGLAND BECAME STANDARD

A standard is a flag or banner used by an individual, country or army as a clear sign of identity. Most countries with a monarchy have a royal standard and many republics will display a traditional military standard, identifying their army or a particular regiment. Originally designed to be shield-shaped, as most emblems were displayed upon the shield of a king or nobleman, the standard was essentially triangular, tapering from a rectangle at one end almost to a point at the other, and was invariably hung vertically. Such flags were inspired by the Roman military standards. Designed to make their armies stand out in battle, these could be used as a rallying point for the troops and were also a good way of intimidating the enemy (see also THE SPREAD EAGLE).

The famous royal standard of England, also known as the Three Lions, has its origins in the Battle of Hastings in 1066. The royal standard prior to this, that of Edward the Confessor (1042–66), is believed to have been a cross surrounded by five martlets (birds). When Edward died childless, influential Anglo-Saxons insisted the king had granted the throne to Harold, an earl who had united Mercia (the Midlands) and led a successful war against the Welsh. Edward's second cousin William of Normandy challenged this, claiming he had been promised the throne by the late king. William considered Harold's coronation a declaration of war and he began to assemble an army in northern France. With a force of nearly 9,000 transported in a fleet of 700 ships, William landed on the southern coast of England on 28 September 1066, set up camp near Hastings and waited for Harold to arrive.

Poor Harold, however, was busy annihilating the Vikings near York in the north of England at the Battle of Stamford Bridge. It took him until 11 October to return to London, regroup and head south to meet William and address the new threat to his kingdom. Harold's standard was first seen by William's scouts on the evening of 13 October and the battle for England began the following morning as both armies clashed, the Norman troops bearing aloft William's standard of two golden lions (see THE WHITE LION) and the English Harold's red dragon. The flags of both sides are depicted on the Bayeux Tapestry, reputedly commissioned by Matilda, William's wife, to commemorate the historic event. As well as depicting the action on the battlefield, the tapestry also illustrates the comet first identified by Edmund Halley (1656–1748), after whom it is named and who predicted its cycle of 75–6 years. Rich in detail, the tapestry also records how Harold was apparently killed, by a single arrow through an eye slit of his helmet, making William the conqueror.

So from that point William's two lions became the royal standard of England. The third lion was added just over a century later by King Richard I, the Lionheart (1157–99), the banner proudly displayed during the Crusades (see THE GEORGE AND DRAGON and THE SARACEN'S HEAD). Standards were important during times of battle as retreating armies would always regroup around the identifying standard, which would be raised high in the air on pikes or lances so that it was clearly visible to all. As a royal or national standard was seen to represent the army itself, it became customary for victors on the battlefield to take the standard of their defeated enemy. In the Middle Ages, the standards of individual knights would be stuck into the ground when camp was set up, enabling soldiers to easily identify the knight to whose army they belonged. Individual standards also had an important role to play during peacetime – at religious festivals, jousting tournaments or during the hunt.

A standard was thus the normal way for a knight to identify himself; his soldiers would declare loyalty to the standard, many even idolizing it. Flags and coats of arms have been used ever since to identify the nobility and hence, in the past, often displayed by innkeepers to align themselves with whichever noble family was in power.

The Star and Garter
THE UNDERWEAR THAT BECAME A DISTINGUISHED MILITARY AWARD

When Edward III came to the throne in 1327, things weren't looking too good for the monarchy. His father,

Edward II, had had a disastrous reign. Bullied by his father, Edward I, he was much more interested in games than in kingship. His wars were unsuccessful, especially in Scotland, where a disastrous defeat at Bannockburn in 1314 had released Scotland from English control. His violent affection for his favourite, Piers Gaveston, led to war with his barons. After they murdered Gaveston, the heartbroken king had kept the remains of his body close to him for a number of weeks before the Church forcibly arranged a burial. Things got so bad that Parliament agreed to his wife Isabella and her lover Roger Mortimer deposing him, although not to his later murder at Berkeley Castle in Gloucestershire, reputedly by introducing a red-hot poker into his rectum (as it was widely believed that he was homosexual).

After the young king had revenged himself on Isabella and Mortimer, mounting a coup to depose them, he needed to drastically improve the public perception of royalty. He also wanted to improve his relationship with the nobility, who had been estranged by his father. He did this by introducing a code of chivalry and evoking the stories of England's legendary king, Arthur. He championed the use of heraldry, which symbolically marked out the powers of the nobility. He chose a new patron saint for England, St George, a dragon-fighting, maiden-rescuing soldier in place of another murdered English king (see THE CROWN AND ARROWS). And in 1344, he resolved to form his own band of knights, like Arthur's, and to install his own Round Table at Windsor Castle. (Arthur had chosen a round table so none of his knights could claim precedence; Edward was equally keen to be seen not to be picking favourites.) Although the table was never actually constructed, Edward did create a special order, consisting of his twenty-four best knights. Each was presented with a blue garter as the king's highest military award.

There are two theories about why this symbol was chosen. According to the first one, the garter was one of the straps a knight would use to secure his armour to his limbs. It was said that Richard the Lionheart, inspired in the twelfth century by the story of St George (see THE GEORGE AND DRAGON), had given garters to his knights for bravery while fighting in the Crusades.

The second, much more popular theory involves underwear rather than armour. The beautiful Countess of Salisbury was dancing near King Edward at Eltham Palace, and was highly embarrassed to find her garter slip from her thigh and land upon the floor in front of the entire court. The tale has it that noble courtiers began sniggering at the sight of a lady's undergarment being revealed to one and all. Rather different from today when you can find young ladies' underwear discarded in just about every bar or nightclub, whether Tom Jones is in town or not. The king, being the gentleman he was, retrieved the garter and placed it upon his own leg with the words '*Honi soit qui mal y pense*' ('Shamed be the person who thinks evil of it'). Both stories reflected well on the king.

A few years later, King Edward, his son the Black Prince and his twenty-four knights led an army of long-bowmen at the Battle of Crécy in 1346, who cut the French army to shreds on the battlefield, completely destroying France's military capability for years to come. The king felt the Order of the Garter had inspired the knights to a famous victory and this great English tradition of awarding the garter to the mightiest of military warriors has continued to this day.

But there has been one significant addition to the award over the last 650 years, introduced by King Charles I during the seventeenth century when he added an eight-point silver medal, or badge, in the shape of a star with the cross of St George at the centre. At this time the garter was also altered and became a four-inch sash to be worn over the shoulder in line with the fashion of the time. From then onwards, the symbolic award has been known as the Star and Garter, or the **Royal Star and Garter**, and the English being the English were bound to honour this highest of honours, the highest in the land, in fact, by naming various alehouses after it as a tribute to some of our great military heroes.

The earliest reference to the Star and Garter being used as the name of an inn or hostelry comes from 1509 when a royal party dined at the village of Shene, a fishing hamlet on the banks of the Thames that later made way for Richmond, and were presented with a bill for their meal by 'the host of the Star and Garter'. Three hundred years later, Charles Dickens became a frequent guest at another Star and Garter in Richmond, marking many important events there, including the birth of his son and over twenty wedding anniversaries. He even held a party at the hotel to celebrate the publication of his novel *David Copperfield* in 1850. The writer continued to meet friends and acquaintances at the hotel until his death in 1870, the same year that the original building was destroyed by fire, although there is no connection. These days the place is called the Petersham Hotel, presumably because it is near the Petersham Road that leads to, you've guessed it, Petersham. Not nearly as interesting a name, is it?

But the Star and Garter in Pall Mall is probably one of the most famous establishments going by this name. It has housed, at various times, the Jockey Club and the Carlton Club, as well as being used to hold the meeting of the committee who revised the cricket laws in 1774 to introduce the 'leg before wicket' (LBW) rule. It was also the venue of a notorious duel in 1765 between Lord Byron, great-uncle of the poet, and his neighbour Mr Chaworth, who had been arguing over the important matter of who had the most game living on their respective country estates in Nottinghamshire. Chaworth died in one of the inn's rooms as a result of his injuries, although he lived long enough to write his will and compose a letter to his mother informing her of the 'unfortunate incident' as he bled to death. Byron survived his wounds but, shunned by society, retired to his Newstead estate where he lived the remainder of his life as a virtual recluse with only his two dogs for company. His sad spirit is said to haunt the grounds to this day. Clearly the wine had been flowing rather too freely at the dinner table in the Star and Garter, Pall Mall, on that particular day.

The Swan with Two Necks

CAN YOU NICK SWANS WHEN YOU OWN THEM?

In the twelfth century, the swan was claimed as a royal bird and only the reigning monarch was permitted to own such a graceful creature, let alone eat one. (They didn't seem too graceful when I was chased into a canal by some swans many years ago, but that's another story.) Since then the English tradition of Swan Upping – a sort of census to check swan numbers – has been carried out

annually during the third week of July. During the ceremony the 'Swan Uppers' of the reigning monarch, currently Queen Elizabeth II, together with those of the Vintners and Dyers (permitted co-owners of the swans), row along the River Thames. Each swan they find along the route is then caught and those collected by the Queen's men are returned to the water, while those caught by the Vintners and Dyers are ringed before being put back.

The Worshipful Company of Vintners was granted a royal charter by Edward III on 13 July 1363, giving them the rights over all wine imports from Gascony in France. The charter also provided rights to sell wine anywhere in England without a licence and the Vintners soon became the most powerful company in the wine trade, raising vast sums of money for the king.

In the sixteenth century Queen Elizabeth I granted rights of ownership of the regal bird both to the Vintners and to the Worshipful Company of Dyers. She ordered that the swans be distinguished from the royal flock by having their beaks marked with two distinctive nicks for the Vintners and one for the Dyers. Over the years, as with so much of the English language, this phrase has been corrupted, leading to the disturbing image of a mutant swan with two necks, although that was not the good Queen's original intention. (Today the swans caught by the Vintners during Swan Upping are marked with a ring on both legs to distinguish them from the royal flock. Those caught by the Dyers are marked with a ring on one leg.) As the Vintners had formed connections with taverns and hostelries around the country, it was common to see a sign of a swan – at first with two nicks on its beak, later with two necks – to advertise their wine.

The Three Horseshoes
ONE WAY TO WARD OFF THE DEVIL

Since most horses are provided with four legs and therefore need four shoes, we can be forgiven for finding something odd about this famous pub name. An old story is told of a pub near a blacksmith's yard where coach drivers or stable lads would pop in for an ale or two while waiting for their steed to have a new shoe fitted. The horse would, naturally, be down to three shoes at that point; hence the pub displayed, as its sign, three horseshoes to indicate to travellers that there was a blacksmith working nearby. The inn further along the road, on the way out of town, was known as the **Four Horseshoes** because by the time the rider, or coach driver, reached it, the horses would have their full quota of footwear.

A single horseshoe has been considered a symbol of good luck for centuries, although there have always been disputes over which way the horseshoe should be hung, up or down, and disputes about which is 'up' or 'down' anyway. According to an old myth, fairies were believed to be afraid of iron. As horseshoes were made of iron and easy to come by, they would be hung above the doors of frightened villagers to keep them safe from wicked fairies.

A similar story about the magical properties of horseshoes concerns Saint Dunstan (909–88). By trade Dunstan was apparently a blacksmith and one day he was approached by the Devil himself because his own fiery charger had lost a shoe. The Devil pleaded with St Dunstan to re-shoe his horse, but instead the man of God nailed the iron shoe to the Devil himself, causing him great pain. St Dunstan then only agreed to remove it after the Devil had promised never to enter any place displaying a horseshoe over the door. And that is apparently a true story. Well, it obviously isn't true because I don't believe St Dunstan was ever a blacksmith. In fact, I doubt he ever did a day's work in his life. What is true is that this story, or one similar, no doubt accounts for how the superstition of a lucky horseshoe evolved. Hence a pub called the Three Horseshoes would appear to suggest the fourth is hanging over the door to ward off the Devil, should he ever decide to drop by for a pint.

The Three Lords

THREE JACOBITE LORDS A-LEAPING . . . TO THEIR DEATHS

It may sound as though this should be yet another pub name celebrating the great and good, but the story behind it is actually rather more bloodthirsty. The three lords in question were rebels who got caught.

The Jacobite Risings were a series of wars started by Scottish rebels who hoped to return the ousted Stuart

The Three Lords

family to the throne of England. Jacobus is the Latin form of the name of the last Stuart king in England, James II (1633–1701), deposed in 1688. What is now known as the First Jacobite Rebellion, the first major uprising, failed at the Battle of Preston in 1715. Then in 1743 James's grandson, Charles Edward Stuart (commonly known as Bonnie Prince Charlie or, by his opponents, as the Young Pretender), was encouraged by the French king, Louis XV, to invade England from the north, while the French (with the blessing of the Pope) invaded from the south.

When a massive storm in the English Channel decimated their fleet, the French invasion plans were cancelled. Nothing daunted, Bonnie Prince Charlie continued with his plans, however, sailing for Scotland in July 1745 where he raised support for his cause among the Scottish clans, triggering what is remembered as the Second

Jacobite Rebellion. Throughout that winter the Scottish rebels and government troops fought bloody battles all over Scotland, culminating in the encounter at Culloden, near Inverness, where the government forces, led by the Duke of Cumberland, crushed Charles's forces on 16 April 1746. Determined to stamp out any remaining support for the Jacobite cause, Cumberland's troops pursued the rebels through the Highlands, killing every battlefield survivor they could find. Indeed, such was his enthusiasm for revenge, Cumberland picked up the nickname of 'the Butcher'. Charles himself escaped, literally Scot-free and dressed as a ladies maid, leaving his supporters behind to face the unpleasant music.

Three Scottish noblemen – William Boyd, 4th Earl of Kilmarnock, Arthur Elphinstone, 6th Baron Balmerinoch, and Simon Fraser, 11th Lord Lovat – were caught and immediately sent for trial in London, where all three were found guilty of high treason. Elphinstone and Boyd were publicly beheaded on Tower Hill in London on 18 August 1746. Unrepentant to the end, Elphinstone made a speech on the scaffold which he ended with the following words: 'If I had a thousand lives, I would lay them all down in the same cause.' Lord Lovat, meanwhile, was beheaded on 9 April the following year, the last man ever to be executed on Tower Hill.

In 1759, during the Seven Years' War, when England and France were yet again pitted against each other, the French planned another invasion, with a force of 100,000 men. Again they were hopeful of Jacobite support from the north and Charles was invited to a meeting with the French foreign minister to discuss the arrangements. When he turned up drunk and belligerent, the unimpressed French swiftly abandoned their plans, and Charles lost for ever the chance to recover the thrones of England and Scotland. Any pub in England or Scotland bearing the name the Three Lords is either demonstrating its support for the Young Pretender or reminding you that, however treacherous the ruling classes can be, at least some of them get their comeuppance (one pub sign has the executioner's axe prominently displayed). But don't let that stop you from enjoying a drink there.

The Three Tuns
WHEN THREE UNITS ARE DEFINITELY MORE THAN ENOUGH . . .

A tun is an old English unit of volume, evolving from a combination of the Roman and Anglo-Saxon systems of weights and measures that were eventually replaced in 1824 by the imperial system. A tun, the equivalent of 256 gallons, was the largest unit of liquid measure for a wine cask. It is four times larger than the **Hogshead**, another well-known name for a pub. In between comes the 128-gallon butt (it's easy to see why that didn't catch on as a pub name).

Three tuns appear on the crest of the Worshipful Company of Vintners, alongside a brace of swans (see THE SWAN WITH TWO NECKS). Hence three tuns displayed outside an inn or tavern demonstrated a connection with the company. The Vintners' motto, '*Vinum Exhilarat Animum*', is a Latin expression meaning 'wine cheers the mind'. I'll drink to that.

The Tickled Trout

DOES TROUT TASTE BETTER WHEN IT'S POACHED?

While the **Trout** is quite common as a pub name, the Tickled Trout is more unusual, although a number of British pubs and hotels are so called. In either case, they are usually situated either on or close to a river. For hundreds of years, boys have been taught how to trap animals for the pot, usually a rabbit or a hare, and poaching has been common in times of economic hardship. Lads from families living near a river or lake would have also been taught trout tickling, the art of catching a fish by hand and a more discreet way of fishing than using a rod and tackle, which might alert the gamekeeper. If done properly, the trout will go into a trance-like state after a minute or so (think of what happens when you rub a dog's stomach) and can then easily be caught and thrown on to the nearest bit of dry land. Despite the risks, ticklers were usually able to escape the long arm of the law, or the short baton of the gamekeeper. Thomas Martindale, in his book *Sport, Indeed* (1901), explains how it was done:

> The fish are watched working their way up the shallows and rapids. When they come to the shelter of a ledge or rock it is their nature to slide under it and rest. The poacher sees the edge of a fin or the moving tail, or maybe he sees neither; instinct, however, tells him a fish ought to be there, so he takes to the water very carefully and stands up near the spot. He then kneels on one knee and passes his hand, turned with fingers up, deftly under the rock until it comes into contact with the fish's tail. Then he begins tickling

with his forefinger, gradually running his hand along the fish's belly and further towards its head until it is under the gills. Then comes a quick grasp, a struggle, and the prize is wrenched out of his natural element, stunned with a blow on the head, and landed in the pocket of a poacher.

But Martindale wasn't the first to record the art of trout tickling. For that we can go right back to the seventeenth century and Shakespeare's *Twelfth Night* (written in around 1601). In the play the lady-in-waiting Maria refers to Malvolio, whom she is conspiring to trick into acting foolishly, as 'the trout that must be caught with tickling' (Act 2, Scene 5).

The illicit practice continues to this day. As recently as 2004, a young man was fined £100 by New Forest magistrates for 'tickling two large sea trout'. The newspaper article, under the headline 'Poacher is Fined for Trout Tickling', explained how the lad had 'waded into the river and caught the fish with his bare hands – a method known as tickling – while they were spawning'.

The Trouble House
(Near Tetbury, Gloucestershire)

A PUB THAT LIVES UP TO ITS NAME

Most pubs, at some point or other, could earn themselves this nickname, especially where I grew up; it goes with the territory. However, this pub, on the road between Tetbury and Cirencester, is peculiarly deserving of the title. It seems to attract trouble like a magnet.

In the early part of the nineteenth century the pub, known then as the **Wagon and Horses**, had become very dilapidated and the landlord decided to rebuild it. But the costs mounted and, halfway through the reconstruction, he fell into such financial difficulty that he hanged himself in despair. The pub was then sold and the new landlord continued with the rebuilding but then he, too, ran into money problems, which so weighed upon him that he also committed suicide, this time by drowning.

This alone, you might think, would be enough to make the place seem a little unlucky, but the troubles didn't stop there. The early nineteenth century was also the period of the Swing Riots (see also THE IRON DUKE), a follow-up to the Luddite Rebellion of 1811–12, in which textile workers, fearing that the growing mechanization of the Industrial Revolution would leave them without work, went about destroying the new looms. Some years later, growing economic hardship following the end of the Napoleonic Wars, together with fears that new farm machinery would threaten their already meagre livelihoods, sparked a similar uprising, this time among agricultural workers in the south of England. In Gloucestershire at around that time, feeling was intense and any new machinery had to be delivered with the utmost secrecy. One day a carter was attempting to deliver a hay-making machine to a farm near the pub. Although he went about it as clandestinely as he could, his mission was discovered. His horses were set loose and his wagon and its troublesome cargo were burned.

With their blood up, the local farm workers went on the rampage, seeking out and destroying any other machinery they could find on farms nearby. Growing in size and hot-headedness, the mob had reached the Wagon and Horses when they were met by the local militia, who eventually quelled the violence, no doubt with a little violence of their own. Following this incident, but evidently not put off by it, a wealthy landowner bought the inn, did it up (amazingly, without falling into debt) and renamed it the Trouble House.

However, it could well be that the unusual name of the pub has nothing to do with the troubles that have beset it over the years. The ground near the pub is regularly flooded and is known historically as the Troubles. Meanwhile the pub itself has lent its name to a couple of other local features. A copse known as Trouble House Cover lies to the north, while not far from the pub was its own railway station. Opened in 1959, the Trouble House Halt was the only station in England built specifically to serve a pub. It closed in 1964 (thanks to Dr Beeching, to whom a coffin filled with empty bottles was sent on the last train from the Halt) but is one of a list of stations commemorated in the song 'The Slow Train' by Flanders and Swann.

The Tumbledown Dick
THE PRODIGAL SON WHO BECAME HEAD OF THE REALM

England's most reluctant ruler, Richard was born on 4 October 1626, the third and least favourite of Oliver Cromwell's sons. As Parliament's forces became increasingly successful in the Civil War, Oliver grew more and more powerful. Richard is believed to have served as a captain in Sir Thomas Fairfax's New Model Army during the late 1640s, although, unlike his father, with little distinction.

After Charles I was beheaded in 1649 (see THE KING'S HEAD), England became a commonwealth. A raft of laws were passed, banning everything from football to Christmas. Drunkenness was seen as ungodly and pubs and revelry generally were frowned upon: the popularity of the new government waned dramatically as a result. In 1653, after wars with Ireland and Scotland, a protectorate was established, with Oliver Cromwell taking the title of Lord Protector of the Commonwealth of England, Scotland and Ireland. He was sworn in with a ceremony in which he wore plain black clothing, rather than any monarchical regalia. However, from this point on previously republican Cromwell signed his name 'Oliver P', standing for 'Oliver Protector' – in a similar style to that used by English monarchs – and it soon became the norm for others to address him as 'Your Highness'.

During the 1650s, Richard's lack of ambition appeared to be troubling his father, to the point where, in 1653, he was not included in his father's 'Barebones Parliament', although his younger brother, Henry, was. When Oliver became Lord Protector in 1653, Richard was offered no public role and instead his dissatisfied father wrote to his father-in-law: 'I would have him mind and understand business, read history and study cosmography and mathematics – these things are good, with subordination to the things of God. Better than idleness or mere outward worldly contents. There are things fit for public service, for which a man is born.' Richard, on the other hand, excelled at idleness, regularly exceeded his allowance, running up embarrassing debts, and, to his father's dismay, ignored religion completely.

But blood finally proved thicker than water and in 1657 Cromwell began to include Richard in affairs of state. In June that year, he was at his father's side during his second installation as Lord Protector, and the following month was given the role of Chancellor of Oxford University. By December, the prodigal son had even become a member of the Council of State. On the day of Oliver Cromwell's death the following year, Richard was informed that he was the new leader, but he wasn't ready to succeed his father.

Unlike Cromwell senior, Richard had no real military or political experience and therefore failed to win any meaningful respect from either the army or Parliament. To make matters worse, he had inherited a regime that was in debt to the tune of £2 million – billions in today's terms – and desperate measures had to be taken. In April 1659, when Parliament threatened cuts to reduce army funding, the generals presented a petition to Richard Cromwell, which he, in turn, passed on to Parliament. Ignoring the petition, Parliament instead passed two resolutions banning any further meetings of army officers without the express permission of the Lord Protector and Parliament, and insisting that officers swear an oath promising never to disrupt or prevent the business of Parliament by force.

The army responded predictably by demanding the dissolution of Parliament. Richard refused but when hostile troops began to gather at St James's in London, he was forced to concede. Having given in to the troops' demands, his next mistake was to refuse an offer of heavily armed support from the French ambassador. By then, he was being ridiculed and mocked by enemies and supporters alike, his nicknames ranging from Queen Dick to Tumble-down Dick.

Before the year was out, so was Richard, having been forced from office, and the monarchy was restored in the shape of King Charles II (see THE ROYAL OAK). In 1660 Richard was forced into exile where, without funds, he lived as a guest of the French court. In 1680 he returned to England and lived extremely quietly in the village of Ches-hunt, Hertfordshire, under the assumed name of John Clarke, dying peacefully at the ripe old age of ninety-one in July 1712. Tumbledown Dick has since become an estab-lished figure of speech used to describe anything that does not, or cannot, stand firmly. Pubs were called Tumbledown Dick in celebration at the return of a hard-drinking, hard-living monarch who enjoyed a joke and a good pub.

The Turk's Head

NOT A HUMAN HEAD BUT A NAUTICAL KNOT?

Some have argued that this name, like THE SARACEN'S HEAD, was inspired by the grim trophies the Crusaders brought back home with them, but there could be another reason, especially if the pub is near the sea. In the villages along the south and west coasts of Britain there is a spe-cial knot used in the construction of fishing nets. It's called the turk's head because it resembles the large, top-heavy turban a Turk was thought to wear.

Generally the signs outside Turk's Heads pubs consist of paintings of swarthy individuals straight from *The Arabian Nights*, but the hotel in Chickerell in Dorset has a picture of the knot hanging outside it instead.

The Turnpike
WHERE ROAD RAGE LED TO RIOTING

There was a time when a pub calling itself the Turnpike was at the cutting edge. A turnpike or toll road is a road or pathway that can be used by travellers for a fee, or toll, usually collected by a town authority responsible for its upkeep. 'Turnpike' can also mean the tollgate itself, the word deriving from a fixed barrier made of sharpened pikes that would have been placed across a road for defence purposes. Later, the turnpike would have been a proper gate that could then be opened to allow passage, closed to prevent it. In the Middle Ages, an era of dirt tracks, toll roads were the motorways, and turnpike inns or taverns the service stations of their day.

In Tudor times each parish was made responsible for maintaining the roads that passed through it. During the late seventeenth century, this piecemeal approach to road maintenance caused acute problems. As trade increased, the growing numbers of heavy carts and carriages led to serious deterioration in the main routes into London but the local parishes didn't have the resources needed for their upkeep. In 1706 Turnpike trusts were introduced by Act of Parliament to fund road maintenance and improvement all over the land. By the mid 1800s, there were over 1,000 Turnpike trusts controlling 30,000 miles of road, to which access was regulated by around 8,000 roadside tollgates and barriers.

Like the Enclosure Acts being enforced at around the same time, in which common land was being taken into private ownership, the new system of toll roads was hugely unpopular. Suddenly communities that had freely used the routes for centuries were being charged to do so. Early legislation gave magistrates powers to punish anyone damaging turnpike property, such as defacing milestones, breaking tollgates or avoiding tolls. Opposition was particularly intense in mountainous regions where good routes were scarce. In 1839, new tolls on old roads sparked the Rebecca Riots in south and mid Wales. Tollgates were vandalized and destroyed by gangs of local men, gatekeepers being told that if they resisted they would be killed. In 1844, the ringleaders were caught and sentenced to transportion to Australia. (To this day there are, however, no pubs called the Turnpike in that part of Britain.)

But the heyday of the turnpikes was a short one. Tollgates began to be perceived as an impediment to free trade. The multitude of small trusts were frequently charged with being inefficient and corrupt, and with the development of the rail network the turnpike system was finally phased out. In 1888 an Act of Parliament gave responsibility for the road networks to the local county and borough councils. With that the tollgates were removed and many of the tollhouses put to other use, turned into travellers' lodges or out-of-town taverns and hotels. Any establishment called the **Tollhouse**, the **Tollgate** or the Turnpike is likely to have once been part of a Turnpike trust.

The Volunteer
WHEN PUBS BECAME ARMY RECRUITING OFFICES

It was in 1804 and midway through the Napoleonic Wars that the British government passed the Volunteer Act.

The legislation was successfully used to raise an army of civilians to defend the coastline from a potential French invasion. But it was fifty years later that the Act was to really come into its own. Tensions flared between the two old adversaries once more after an assassination attempt on Emperor Napoleon III on 14 January 1858. The French blamed the English after evidence that would-be assassin Felice Orsini had travelled to England to have his bombs made. British military resources, deployed in the Crimea and other parts of Europe, were already over-stretched and there was every chance that Britain itself could be left defenceless if further conflict broke out.

When it did, thanks to the Franco-Austrian War of 1859, the British secretary of state for war issued a letter to all the county lieutenants of England authorizing them to form a volunteer rifle corps, especially around the coastal towns, most in need of defence if invasion was imminent. Using local inns and taverns displaying a 'volunteer' sign, the men were recruited in huge numbers, leading to the formation of volunteer regiments all over the country, otherwise known as the Riflemen. Alfred Tennyson captured the mood of the country in his own poetic call for volunteers, 'Riflemen Form', which was published in *The Times* (the first and last verse printed here):

> There is a sound of thunder afar,
> Storm in the south that darkens the day,
> Storm of battle and thunder of war,
> Well, if it do not roll our way.
> Form! form! Riflemen form!
> Ready, be ready to meet the storm!
> Riflemen, riflemen, riflemen form!
>
> Form, be ready to do or to die!
> Form in freedom's name and the Queen's!
> True, that we have a faithful ally,
> But only the devil knows what he means!
> Form! form! Riflemen form!
> Ready, be ready to meet the storm!
> Riflemen, riflemen, riflemen form!

By 1862 the Volunteer Force numbered almost 170,000 men, fully trained and ready to defend their country in the face of the threat of French invasion. This significant military presence would certainly have helped deter Napoleon III, who took the decision not to attack, or even threaten Great Britain again.

In 1907 the Territorial and Reserve Forces Act merged the Volunteer Force and the Yeomanry into the Territorial

Force. They were famously used as a recruiting vehicle at the start of the First World War to drum up recruits for Kitchener's Army (see THE LORD KITCHENER). Deeming conscription to be a bad idea for the morale of the country, Kitchener geared his recruitment campaign to the notion that a young man was more likely to volunteer his services if he knew he would be training, marching and fighting with his friends and family. And so the Pals Battalions were formed all over Britain, entire villages and towns posted together in one single battalion and sent to the front lines.

In retrospect, this was a disastrous policy, as tragically proven on 1 July 1916 at the River Somme in northern France, in what became known as the Somme Offensives or the Battle of the Somme. It was here the Allied forces attempted to break through the German lines along a twelve-mile stretch of the river and in just one day suffered nearly 60,000 casualties, nearly 20,000 of which were fatal. The Pals Battalions suffered horrendously as just one shell, or machine-gun attack, could deprive an entire village of its able-bodied young men. The Leeds Pals lost 750 men in just a few hours, while Grimsby and Sheffield both lost nearly 500 men over a similar period of time. Inhabitants of the small town of Accrington were to mourn nearly 600 deaths that took place on that day alone. As Percy Holmes, the brother of one victim, stated to the *Accrington Observer* many years later: 'I recall when the news came through to Accrington that the Pals had been wiped out. I don't think there was a street in Accrington and district that didn't have their blinds drawn, and the bell at Christ Church tolled all day long.'

Prior to the fighting, people had been caught up in the

patriotism and enthusiasm of volunteering for a just cause, but poor military strategy during the war resulted in the devastation of entire communities. Unsurprisingly, the Pals' experiment was never repeated.

After 1920 the Territorial Force became known as the Territorial Army, which engages in military activities to this day. The TA continues to be a volunteer force, its history traceable to the days when young men would go to the local tavern with the 'volunteer' sign displayed outside and offer to serve and protect their country. They and those that came after them are one of the reasons we can sleep soundly in our beds at night, and why French or German is not our national tongue.

J. D. Wetherspoon
HOW GEORGE ORWELL'S IDEAL PUB INSPIRED A CHAIN REACTION

This renowned chain of pubs, stretching country-wide, was founded back in 1979 when twenty-four-year-old law graduate Tim Martin opened his first pub in Colney Hatch Lane, London. From modest beginnings Martin's company has grown into one of the largest independent pub and hotel chains in Britain. Although not old – certainly not in comparison with most of the other pubs in this book – J. D. Wetherspoon, with its distinctive name and revenue of over £900 million a year, seems well worth investigating.

Interestingly, literary inspiration has played a large part in the formation of the pub chain. In an essay written by George Orwell for the *London Evening Standard* and published on 9 February 1946, the author of *Nineteen Eighty-Four* describes his ideal pub, the Moon Under Water. Inspired by Orwell's description of the pub's agreeable atmosphere and his comment that the place was 'always quiet enough to talk', the Wetherspoon group took the decision not to play the loud music once expected in all English pubs of an evening. Despite this, Wetherspoon's Orwellian principle of providing cheap food and drink for the masses has inevitably led to the pubs becoming a magnet for hard-up students, and it is in the university towns that they have chiefly flourished. Orwell's perfect pub has also lent its name to a number of pubs in the chain, all called the **Moon Under Water**. By contrast, other Wetherspoon pubs have been carefully named after local heroes or historic events. Hence in Rotherham, for instance, the Wetherspoon pub on the High Street is called the **Corn Law Rhymer** after Ebenzer Elliott, a local iron merchant who expressed his indignation at the unfair Corn Laws (see THE IRON DUKE) by writing a volume of verse called, naturally enough, *Corn Law Rhymes*, and published in 1831.

And so to the question of where the distinctive name – J. D. Wetherspoon – comes from. The idea for the name appears to have occurred to Tim Martin during his first ever night as a pub manager. On that evening, the customers started fighting with each other and Martin found he was unable to control the crowd. When a chair went flying through a window, the young manager was immediately reminded of a former lecturer of his, who, like him, had been unable to control an unruly crowd, in his case a classroom of bored students. He was the same tutor who had written on Martin's report card: 'Tim will probably amount to nothing.' His name was Wetherspoon, to which Tim added the initials 'J. D.' in honour of his favourite television character of the 1970s, J. D. Hogg, from *The Dukes of Hazzard*. And that, believe it or not, is a true story.

The Wheatsheaf

HOW MAN EVOLVED FROM THE BEASTS ... THROUGH
DRINKING BEER

Except at harvest festivals, a wheatsheaf is a rare sight today, when the fields after harvest are dotted with vast straw bales rather than stooks of hand-gathered sheaves or bundles of wheat. There are many traditions associated with the harvest of former times. In some regions the farmers believed that bad spirits resided in the corn and so the last sheaf to be harvested would be trampled on the ground to chase the sprits away. By contrast, the Devon ceremony of 'Crying the Neck' involved the last sheaf or 'neck' being raised into the air by way of ritual celebration. Elsewhere strands of wheat would be woven into a 'corn dolly' that was kept safe for luck until seed-sowing the following year, when the ears of grain would be ploughed back into the soil in order to bless the new crop. Wheat and other cereals have always been a vital crop, providing bread to fill the stomach and, much more importantly, beer to lift the spirits.

Beer, mostly brewed from malted barley (see THE MALTINGS) but also made from wheat, maize or rice, is one of the oldest manufactured drinks in the world. It was first recorded in the written history of ancient Egypt and Mesopotamia around 5000 BC, and archaeological evidence goes back a couple of millennia before that. So, at around nine thousand years old, beer and its history should clearly be included in any book touching on the history of mankind, especially one concerned with the history of the places in which beer was drunk.

The chronicle of beer can be traced back to the earliest civilizations, of the Chinese, Egyptians and Mesopotamians, who were the first people to actually organize their societies and communicate with each other without pointing and shouting. It is thought that the Sumerians in southern Mesopotamia were the first to brew beer after, it is assumed, some grain became moist and began to ferment. Very soon they realized they could repeat the process as often as they wanted, and before long, no doubt, they were all under the influence of their new discovery and pointing and shouting at each other again. This took place around nine thousand years ago, and mankind has been adapting and refining the process ever since. Odd, then, that even after all these years of research and learning from the practice of others, the Australians are still unable to produce a drinkable beer.

In Mesopotamia, during the second millennium before the birth of Christ, a narrative poem, *The Epic of Gilgamesh*, was written to explain how man evolved. Enkidu, a hairy primitive who ate only grass and drank only the milk of wild animals, wanted to test his power against the demigod Gilgamesh. Seeking to learn about his enemy, Gilgamesh sent a prostitute to spend a week with the wild man to teach him about civilization. Among other things, she taught him how to eat bread and drink beer as it was the 'custom of the kingdom', so Enkidu drank seven cups of beer, after which his heart soared, he cleaned himself up and became a civilized human being. Although these days, after seven cups of beer, that process seems to happen in reverse. Indeed, perhaps after seven cups of the ancient ale, Enkidu wisely had an afternoon nap before going out for a mountain-goat madras in the evening.

There is evidence that all the ancient civilizations drank some form of beer; the Babylonians even had laws establishing beer rations. For the record, it was the priests who received the most, around a gallon a day, probably accounting for all those visions they kept having. Beer was popular among the Romans before wine-making took over, when it was considered a barbarian drink. The Romans occupying Britannia noted how the Celtic Druids drank ale made from barley, fermented yeast and water. They tried to introduce their wine to the Druids, but without success. And that state of affairs seems to have continued as, by the end of the Middle Ages, beer remained Britain's most popular drink, drunk from breakfast through until night-time, just like it is around most football stadiums today.

During the fifteenth century, merchants began importing European hops as a new type of bittering agent to temper the sweetness of the malted grain (previously flavoured with chequer berries – see THE BUSH), and what was referred to as 'ale' was now called 'beer'. This was when a distinction grew between lager and the traditional bitter, which it seems, even now, only the British can stomach. It was during this period that innkeepers would display a picture of a wheatsheaf outside their alehouses to advertise traditional English 'real ales' were available, and not that European 'rubbish'.

At nearly nine thousand years old, beer drinking is as old as civilization itself. Indeed, as Enkidu found out, beer quite possibly did much of the civilizing. Although you wouldn't always think that when walking through most English towns of an evening, stepping over half-eaten kebabs and sleeping teenagers, when the traditional pastime of drinking beer is taking place.

The White Hart
SYMBOL OF A KING WITH LITTLE HEART

Something that used to trouble me as a child was why the White Hart at Pirbright, close to where I grew up, was spelled without an 'e'. And what would a white heart be in any case?

If the pub had been called the **White Stag** instead, all would have been clear. For a hart is in fact an adult male deer, especially a red deer. A white one would be rare indeed, sufficiently rare to go questing after it, as Sir Gawain does in one of the legends of King Arthur (see also THE GREEN MAN), when a white hart runs through the hall at Camelot. Interestingly, the word 'deer' – related to the modern German word *Tier*, meaning 'animal' – originally meant a wild animal of any kind, as opposed to a farmed one. Over time, it came to mean one specific creature. (Likewise the word 'venison' applied to all wild game, not just the meat from a deer.) The town of Hertford (pronounced 'Hartford') grew up around a river crossing point for animals; its name clearly means 'the place deer cross the river'. And all this, in turn, means when we talk about the White Hart a deer is what is referred to, and the name has nothing to do with the blood-pumping organ in the middle of our chests.

Of course, that now raises the other question, why so many pubs and hotels are named after the rare and elusive animal. The reason for this is that the white deer or hart was used by English king Richard II (1367–1400) as his heraldic symbol, and members of his household and court would all display the white hart in one form or another. Innkeepers and tavern owners would also display the image on their signs to show allegiance to the king. This would have been a wise move in such turbulent times. Richard II, who came to the throne as a child (see THE RED LION), was the monarch famous for crushing the first poll tax riots in 1381, better known as the Peasants' Revolt (see JACK STRAW'S CASTLE). After the revolt was quashed, the heartless (with an 'e') king broke all the promises he had made and sent a militia through the countryside to seek out any remaining rebels. Having a sign outside your pub with the king's symbol painted prominently upon it was a good way of ensuring that you and your clientele of revolting peasants avoided royal retribution.

The White Lion

EMBLEM OF THE FIRST YORKIST KING OF ENGLAND

Regarded as the king of the beasts and a creature of dauntless courage, the lion has long been used as a symbol of royalty. In heraldic terms, lions tend to be golden and sometimes red, but rarely white. The royal coat of arms of the United Kingdom consists of a shield display-

The White Lion

ing various lions, two sets of three golden and one red (see THE STANDARD and THE RED LION), the shield supported on one side by another golden lion, for England, and on the other by a silver unicorn, for Scotland (see also THE LION AND THE UNICORN). The three formerly golden lions from the royal coat of arms also appear on the badge worn by our national football team. These lions aren't white, either, but dark blue.

Edward IV (1442–83), son of Richard, 3rd Duke of York (see THE ROSE AND CROWN), was a hugely popular king of the York dynasty. He was a brilliant general and talented politician; indeed, had he not died when his son and heir was only twelve, the house of Lancaster might not have won the War of the Roses. Edward used a white lion as his personal emblem, which is almost certainly why so many English pubs, hotels, lanes and even shopping centres bear the name the White Lion today.

Edward IV in turn inherited the symbol from his grand-mother Anne de Mortimer, which accounts for why some pubs are called the **White Lion of Mortimer**. The lion, depicted carrying a shield bearing the white rose of York encircled by a golden sun, appeared on the Great Seal of Edward IV, more recently used by George VI (1895–1952) when he was Duke of York.

The remains of lions were found buried in the moat at the Tower of London in 1936. The bones – of the Barbary lion from north-west Africa where lions are now extinct – were recently carbon-dated to Edward IV's reign. They would have been part of a royal menagerie at the Tower, consisting of exotic animals and housed in the Bulwark Tower, specially built for the purpose. It was later renamed the Lion Tower but was largely demolished, with the exception of the Lion Gate, after the animals were removed in 1835 on the orders of the Duke of Wellington (see THE IRON DUKE).

The Widow's Son
(Bow, London)

WHERE 'VINTAGE' APPLIES TO THE FOOD NOT THE DRINK

In the early nineteenth century, a widow lived in a small cottage on the Devon Road in Bow, east London. As Easter approached one year, she was looking forward to seeing her only son, a sailor in the Royal Navy, who was due home from his first voyage at sea. As it was Good Friday, his mother baked him a hot-cross bun to celebrate his homecoming. It was then widely believed that buns baked on Good Friday had miraculous powers (helped by the cross) and would never go mouldy. Hence their presence in the house was considered lucky and protective. The following day she waited impatiently at the front gate, looking up and down the road in the hope of catching sight of him, but as dusk fell she realized he was unlikely to come that day. Easter Day came and went and there was still no sign of him. The days turned into weeks, the weeks into months, and still he did not come.

The widow kept the bun she had baked for her son, threading it on to a cord and hanging it from a beam, for the day he finally did return. Each new day came and went, much as the last, and each day the old woman stood at the gate, looking up and down Devon Road, hoping to see her son, but he never arrived. Eventually news came that he had been lost at sea, presumed dead, although no body had been recovered that could be returned to his grieving mother. So the widow clung to the thin belief that her son was still alive and would eventually find his way home. To mark the passing of each year she baked him a hot-cross bun, threaded it on to the cord with the other buns and hung it back on the beam. She was never to see her son again and when she died her cottage was knocked down and a fine new tavern built in its place.

The story goes that the workmen, discovering the string of buns, wanted to show respect to the old widow by hanging them in the new bar, and the new landlord, upon hearing the tragic tale, decided to keep the buns on show and named his pub the Widow's Son in honour of the lost boy and his devoted mother. Each year since 1848, when a pub was first built on the site, successive landlords have continued his tradition of inviting a member of the

Royal Navy to add a hot-cross bun to the pile, now stored in a net hanging from the ceiling, still on display in the main bar and now numbering over two hundred buns. But if you're hungry, I'd definitely advise you to stick to the sandwiches.

The Woolpack
THE TRADE THAT HELPED MAKE BRITAIN GREAT

For centuries the wool trade was an important part of the English economy. The Domesday Book, the great survey of England commissioned by William the Conqueror and completed in 1086, records how the industry was already thriving at that time, with flocks of up to 2,000 sheep. Many English towns grew as a result of the wool trade, becoming flourishing centres of production. By 1260 records show that hundreds of flocks had over 8,000 sheep, each managed by as many as a dozen full-time shepherds. By the reign of Edward I (1239–1307), wool had become the country's major export to Europe. It was also a significant source of income for the king, who in 1275 sought to regulate the industry by introducing a form of export tax called the 'Great Custom'.

As a part of the new regulations, Edward demanded that that woolpacks, previously random in size, were made uniform, at around 240 pounds each in weight. This became the standard. The Great Custom, in turn, became the cornerstone of the English tax system, in the first instance helping to raise money to fund the Hundred Years' War (see also THE AGINCOURT and JACK STRAW'S CASTLE). Other forms of taxation and regulation were introduced over the years, while the smuggling of sheep or wool out of the country (known as 'owling' because it was carried out at night) attracted severe punishment. Anyone caught smuggling would have his left hand cut off, the hand then being nailed in a public place to act as a deterrent to any other would-be offenders.

Such was the importance of the wool industry that from the fourteenth century the presiding officer of the House of Lords (formerly the Lord Chancellor, since 2006 the Lord Speaker) has sat upon a large red seat stuffed with wool. Known as the Woolsack, this serves as a symbolic reminder of how it was wealth from the wool trade that funded, and helped found, our once great nation.

There are Woolpack hotels, inns and taverns scattered all over England, but the most famous of all is a fictional one: the pub in a British soap opera that has been running since 1972, *Emmerdale*. The village of Esholt in west Yorkshire was used as a set to film the programme between 1976 and 1998. For the purpose of the series, the village pub changed its name from the Commercial Inn to the Woolpack, becoming a major tourist attraction in the process.

The World's End

A CITY BOUNDARY OR A SIXTEENTH-CENTURY PROPHECY?

The popularity of the World's End as a pub name is likely to lie in the fact that it makes such a great response to someone asking where to go for a drink; 'Let's go to The World's End'. (That's how far you'd go when you really need a drink.)

The World's End

The phrase may indicate the end of the world in a geographical sense. And this would appear to apply in the case of the World's End in Edinburgh. The pub is situated where part of the city wall once ran, marking the end of the rest of the world and the beginning of the Scottish capital (the main gate or entrance to the city was located nearby). The other sense of the phrase is, of course, the ending of our planet, as predicted with disturbing regularity by prophets and soothsayers down the ages.

One of the most famous of such doom-mongers – and one commemorated in many a pub name – may be traced to the unlikely spot of Knaresborough, in Yorkshire, previously best known as the place where the murderers of Thomas à Becket fled after killing him in 1170. It is here that Ursula Southeil (*c.*1488–1561) was born. Better known as Mother Shipton, she is the prophetess responsible for many startlingly accurate predictions that put Nostradamus firmly in the league of 'having a bit of a stab at it'.

Among the events that she predicted are the Great Plague of London and the Great Fire – Samuel Pepys even refers to her in his diary. She also predicted the English Civil War and warned of the threat from the Spanish and their Armada (see THE GOLDEN HIND and THE LORD HOWARD), and she publicly declared that Cardinal Wolsey, Archbishop of York, would never actually enter the town. Legend has it that Henry VIII's right-hand man then vowed to 'have the witch burned' when he finally arrived in York, and was actually on his way there in 1530 when he was ordered back to London to be tried for treason.

Legend also has it that Ursula Southeil was born in a cave near the River Nidd and that the Devil was her father. She was born terribly deformed and smelling of sulphur, and a mighty crack of thunder shook the town at her birth. Which sounds suspiciously like a story put about by the real father, Lord Somebody-or-other or Baron Nothing-to-do-with-me-your-honour. At the age of twenty-four she apparently married a carpenter called Toby Shipton, although they had no children, which is perhaps not surprising as Mother Shipton has been described as hideously ugly with a hunched back, large hooked nose, facial hair and missing teeth.

Since the 1640s, many books have been written about her, each one lauding her achievements with the benefit of hindsight. She apparently prophesied Henry VIII's victory over the French at the Battle of the Spurs in 1513 and the Dissolution of the Monasteries in 1536–41. Published after her death was a series of poems predicting many, at that time, unimaginable events such as man in flight; ships made of iron and steel; carriages without a horse; gold in an as yet unknown land; England and France fighting as one; and messages sent through the air in an instant. She also predicted the eventual destruction of mankind and subsequent ending of the world. However, she made the mistake of putting a date on this, one that terrified the Victorians but which we should find rather less scary:

> The world to an end shall come
> In eighteen hundred and eighty-one.

Hence the popularity of the name since then: the only World's End any of us is likely to encounter is a pub. I'll drink to that.

Pubs Named in Honour of Famous Racehorses

The links between alcohol and racing are well known. But something that has surprised me in my research is just how many pubs there are named after racehorses. And it's not simply grateful owners and gamblers who become publicans; it turns out that quite a few jockeys retire to run pubs, funded in many cases by their winnings from riding a particular horse. This may also explain why so many pub landlords are built along Napoleonic lines. Small they may be, but, like elephants, jockeys have long memories, and many have named their pub after the horse that got them there. Here are ten of my favourites. (There are many more, of course.)

The Alfisidora
(Bishop Burton, North Humberside)

This rural pub on the road between Hull and York is named after a three-year-old chestnut filly that won the St Leger in 1814. Legend recalls how the local squire staked his entire fortune on the horse and then renamed the village inn after his famous victory. If that is true, then his bank manager and heart specialist probably also erected statues in honour of the horse and we can only imagine how his wife must have reacted. The spirited racehorse was almost certainly named after the Lady Altisidora who teases Don Quixote so unmercifully in Cervantes's famous novel.

The Arkle Manor
(Betchworth, Surrey)

This traditional country pub was renamed in 1970 after an Irish thoroughbred who became a byword for extreme speed in the mid 1960s. Arkle beat the previously unstoppable Mill Reef in 1964 to win the first of three consecutive Cheltenham Gold Cups by over twenty lengths, capturing the hearts of the nation in the process. When this was followed by a couple of Hennessy Gold Cups, a King George VI Chase and an entire year of unbeaten runs, the horse became a sporting legend. The racing authorities even took the unprecedented step of devising two weight systems in the Irish Grand National – one to be used when Arkle was running and one when he wasn't. Arkle won the 1964 race by only one length but he was carrying two and half stone more than his rivals. Calls of 'Arkle for President' only strengthened his fame and he was simply known as 'Himself'. Fan mail from all over the world addressed to 'Himself, Ireland' would usually reach his stables. The Irish joked that drinking Guinness twice a day was the source of his strength. So there should be no doubts about the beer of choice at any pub named after him.

The Blue Peter
(Peterborough, Cambridgeshire)

A Blue Peter is a blue flag with a white square in the centre traditionally raised by a ship to signal that it is preparing to set sail. Introduced in 1750 and originally consisting of a blue flag with six white balls raised, it soon became part of the international code of signals as the signal for 'P'. In the old phonetic alphabet 'Peter' was the word for the letter 'P', replaced in today's alphabet by the word 'Papa'. The popular children's programme, first broadcast in 1958, was so named because it intended to 'set sail on a voyage of discovery with its young viewers'. Many pubs, especially those on the coast, are named after the naval signal, but at least one takes its name from a racehorse that won the Derby in 1939. Blue Peter was one of the finest Derby winners of all time and, had the outbreak of the Second World War not meant all the key races were cancelled, could have gone on to win the Triple Crown (the Derby, the 2,000 Guineas Stakes and the St Leger).

The Brigadier Gerard
(Eastleigh, Hampshire, and York)

Winning eighteen out of nineteen races between 1970 and 1972, Brigadier Gerard became one of the world's most popular racehorses – especially among the sort of people who invest the housekeeping money with their bookmakers. The Brigadier Gerard Stakes at Sandown is named in his honour, as are these two pubs.

The horse was named after Brigadier Etienne Gerard, a fictional hussar in the French army during the Napoleonic Wars (see THE PRINCE BLUCHER for a real-life hussar from that time), the hero of a series of short comic stories by Sir Arthur Conan Doyle. Bored with his omniscient creation Sherlock Holmes, Conan Doyle enjoyed creating the complete antithesis to the famous detective: a hero with very little sense who bravely blunders through the events of world history. Confidently believing himself to be the world's greatest lover, swordsman, soldier and gentleman, Brigadier Gerard has all kinds of ridiculous adventures generally on horseback, due, all too often, to a very French misunderstanding of the English and their customs. One well-known story has him joining a hunt with the English army; when he catches up with the fox he kills it with his sabre, much to the horror (and barely suppressed amusement) of the English officers.

The Dr Syntax Inn
(New Ridley and Prudhoe, Northumberland)

Dr Syntax was the hero of a series of highly popular cartoons by the English caricaturist Thomas Rowlandson (1756–1827). *The Tour of Dr Syntax in Search of the Picturesque* (1813), *The Second Tour of Dr Syntax in Search of Consolation* (1820) and *The Third Tour of Dr Syntax in Search of a Wife* (1821) proved to be so popular with the public that a Newcastle racehorse was named after him. The horse went on to win the Derby in 1820, inspiring the name of two Northumberland pubs in the process. Syntax, in case you're wondering, is, as some writers will be able to tell you, the correct arrangement of words in a sentence – or the art of structuring sentences properly. For example, 'The old grey racehorse that won the Derby' is good syntax; 'The grey old racing horse who lost' is not.

The Eclipse

Just as most inns called THE BLUE PETER are named after the naval flag, so most Eclipse pubs are named after the moment when the sun is covered by the moon and the sky turns black. However, a few are named in honour of a champion racehorse born during the eclipse of the sun in 1764. Eclipse was undefeated during his entire career and, legend has it, without ever being spurred on or whipped. The expression 'Eclipse first and the rest nowhere', popular at the time, is said to have its origins in the phrase commonly uttered by the horse's owner, Captain Dennis O'Kelly, when placing bets for a race. The Eclipse Stakes (UK and Canada), Prix Eclipse (France) and the Eclipse Award (America) are races all named in honour of the famous stallion.

The Flying Childers
(Matlock, Derbyshire)

Born in 1714 and a direct descendant of one of the three Arabian stallions that fathered the modern thoroughbred bloodline, the Flying Childers is often described as the first truly great racehorse. Named after his trainer, Colonel Leonard Childers, the horse was also often called the Devonshire Childers in deference to his owner, the Duke of Devonshire. The horse won only a few major races, but at such a canter the duke retired him to stud. This was despite receiving an offer of the horse's weight in gold from a rival owner, such was the value placed on

Childers. The stallion then went on to sire many other champion racehorses, no doubt earning the wily duke several times the animal's weight in gold in the end. However, it's hardly surprising that the version of the horse's name chosen for a pub concentrates on his speed and grace rather than the business acumen of his owner.

The Flying Fox
(Colchester, Essex)

Neither a tropical fish nor a fruit bat (although it could be either of these), this Flying Fox is another famous racehorse, the Triple Crown champion of 1899. Owned by the 1st Duke of Westminster, Flying Fox was a notoriously volatile creature and very difficult to handle. He was retired to stud after becoming only the eighth horse in history to win the prestigious Triple Crown during an undefeated season. Following the duke's death that same year, he was sold at auction, purchased for a record 37,500 guineas (£35,714). Exported to France by his new owner, he sired many other champions and first-class winners before his death in 1911. His skeleton is on display in the museum at the Château de Saumur and there is a memorial of him at Eaton Stud in Cheshire.

The Little Wonder

Little Wonder made horse-racing history in 1840 by winning the Derby at underdog odds of fifty to one. Besides inspiring pubs to be named in his honour, the horse also lent his name to another sporting legend. Bare-knuckle boxer and racing enthusiast Thomas Sayers (1826–65) adopted the nickname during his eleven-year fighting career between 1849 and 1860. Boxing was as popular as racing but completely unregulated and very violent: matches went on until one assailant was knocked unconscious, which could take several hours. Consequently, it was illegal and the fights had to be held clandestinely: Sayers's first proper fight was fought barefoot at night on Wandsworth Common so that he could escape more easily through the mud if the police arrived.

No taller than a jockey, standing at only five foot eight inches in his bare feet and weighing under eleven stone, Sayers was also known as the Napoleon of the Prize Ring. In 1857 he became the first boxer to be declared World Heavyweight Champion when he knocked out the Tipton Slasher (William Perry). Sayers's last fight, in 1860 in America, was the first international boxing match fought by an Englishman. After thirty-seven damaging, bare-knuckle rounds against John C. Heenan, his American opponent, Little Wonder began to tire and his supporters invaded the ring, prompting the police to follow suit, and several arrests were made. An exhausted Sayers was persuaded to retire (a public subscription of £3,000 was collected for him, a huge sum of money in those days but reflecting his great popularity) and he spent the last five years of his life frittering away his pension in the pubs and taverns of London. He became a familiar figure on the streets of the capital, always accompanied by his enormous dog, Lion. When he died, aged just thirty-nine, 10,000 people attended his funeral. He is buried in Highgate Cemetery, with a statue of Lion lying across his tomb.

The Seabiscuit Inn
(Wells, New York)

Seabiscuit was the champion thoroughbred that in 1936 became a symbol of hope to an American people knocked sideways by the Great Depression. Appropriately for those lean economic times, the names of both Seabiscuit and his sire, Hard Tack, are derived from naval expressions to describe a seaman's unappetizing daily 'bread' ration while on board ship. Seabiscuit lost many times before he found his winning streak, and his pluck, stamina and trick of snatching victory from the jaws of defeat proved inspirational. The subject of a bestselling book (2001) and a film nominated for an Oscar in 2003, Seabiscuit has become the most famous American racehorse of all time.

Further Reading

As I said in the introduction my only regret is that there are so many pub names and stories I haven't had the space to write about. Here are some entertaining books (only one of them written by me) that will tell you more:

The Local: the History of the English Pub by Paul Jennings (2007)

The Wordsworth Dictionary of Pub Names

Licensed to Sell: The History and Heritage of the Public House by Geoffrey K. Brandwood (2004)

About the history of beer:
Man walks into a pub: a sociable history of beer by Pete Brown (2004)

About local legends and popular history:
The Lore of the Land: A Guide to England's Legends by Jennifer Westwood and Jacqueline Simpson (2005)

London Lore by Steve Roud (2008)

Pop Goes the Weasel: The Secret Meanings of Nursery Rhymes by Albert Jack (2008)

And about the pub's influence on sport:

Can We Have Our Balls Back Please: How the British invented sport and then (almost) forgot how to play by Julian Norridge (2008)

Index

(**Bold** indicates principal entry)